CANADA AND THE NEW INTERNATIONAL ECONOMY

T0335252

CANADA AND THE NEW INTERNATIONAL ECONOMY

Three Essays

Edited by

H. E. ENGLISH

Published in co-operation with
Carleton University by
University of Toronto Press

University of Toronto Press
Diamond Anniversary 1961

Introduction

THIS BOOK COMPRISES in slightly revised form three papers presented as public lectures at Carleton University in Ottawa on February 21, 22, and 23, 1961. A concluding section has been added, highlighting the main points made by the lecturers and including some of the recorded discussion which followed the lectures.

The purpose of the series was to relate Canada's current trade position and policy problem to historical and current international efforts to take advantage of the universally acknowledged benefits of specialization and exchange among nations and regions. All of the authors are economists but some care has been taken to choose economists who, while making no pretence at knowing the art of politics better than its practitioners, have long endeavoured in their writings to take account of other social objectives and of the limitations placed upon economic policy by immediate political necessities.

In the matter of international trade, as in other economic matters, the relevant issue is ultimately whether international trade can contribute to the achievement of our most cherished social objectives. Among our principal objectives are peace, prosperity, and national identity. We have a right to expect that economists will throw light on the means of achieving these. Today in Canada (as elsewhere) there is not much disagreement with the proposition that trade should lead to prosperity and to peace and one might have thought that this would be a rather impressive argument for searching out every conceivable means of expanding trade. But many Canadians remain troubled and uncertain. They seem to say: "If we lose our opportunity to be Canadians what is the use of being prosperous?" and even sometimes, "What is the use of survival if it is not part and parcel of national survival?" This kind of implicit priority places a high premium on nationhood and would seem to presume a definition of national purpose somewhat better than that associated with the empty symbolism of the past, or the pathetic introversion of the present.

The very least that we might expect of a nationalism that would deserve such high priority in the last half of the twentieth century is that it would command respect in other nations, that it would, for example, promote peace rather than the reverse. How can foreign trade policy play a part in building such a version of nationhood? Is it possible that a policy of maintaining and increasing industry through protection will give Canada an increased ability to speak and act as an independent nation on the world stage? Does economic self-sufficiency make possible a stronger voice in world politics? Or on the other hand, may it not be possible to command more respect abroad by acknowledging economic interdependence and (to put it in its crudest form) by exploiting the willingness to trade associated with such a policy as a means of commanding the friendship of others, and perhaps also to use some of the resulting gain in national real income as a means of assisting those still in process of economic development? If, as Disraeli is alleged to have said, "Trade is not a principle, it is an expedient," let us be sure that it is expedient to the achievement of the best national aspirations.

It is in this ambitious context that the papers are presented to the reader, not because the authors believe that they can offer a last word on issues that are characteristically changeable, but because they are confident that any other context would be misleading and unsatisfactory.

In the first instance the lectures were sponsored by the Department of Economics at Carleton University. We are grateful to The Dean's Alumni Fund for University Development and to the Institute for Canadian Studies for the financial assistance which made possible this publication.

Ottawa
July, 1961   H. E. ENGLISH

Contents

CANADA AND THE NEW INTERNATIONAL ECONOMY

The Historical Perspective: Nineteenth-Century Trade Theory and Policy

H. SCOTT GORDON[1]

Carleton University

ON ONE OCCASION, as a sort of perverse academic hobby, I began collecting all the instances in which a period in history was described, either contemporaneously or in retrospect, as an "age of transition." I abandoned my collection when it appeared certain that all of recorded history would be covered by this description. Despite the apparent agelessness of this *cliché*, I do feel that it has some significance when people are very aware of the transitional character of their own times. It signifies, I think, that people are exceptionally conscious of the fact that they must make certain important and perhaps irrevocable choices or decisions in their social and political affairs—conscious that they stand, to use another *cliché*, "at the crossroads of decision."

This is certainly not the first time in Canadian history that our external economic policy has occupied the centre of the Canadian political stage. But I venture to say that there has been no other time when it has been more important for Canada to decide not only what our own policy should be but also what influence we will try to exert on the policies of the rest of the world. We have come to a crucial point, not only in *Canadian* economic development but also in *world* economic development—and not only in world *economic* development but also in world *political and social* development.

[1] In preparing this revised version of the lecture, the author has been indebted to Dr. David M. L. Farr, Professor of History at Carleton University, for his comments on several points.

When the history of the mid-twentieth century is written, I wonder how future historians will characterize our time—aside from the fact that it was "an age of transition?" Perhaps they will look to the creation of nation states out of the old colonial territories and call it "The Triumph of Nationalism." Or perhaps the new trade groupings of Europe and elsewhere will turn out to be restrictive and protectionist and the future economic historians will write our chapter as "The Slightly Enlarged Isolationism." Or will it turn out that the Common Market, the Free Trade Area, the United Nations, I.M.F., F.A.O., and a host of other international developments were the beginnings of something grander—more generous, more cosmopolitan, even more utopian—and the future historian will be able to call our age "The Beginnings of World Community?" This is the kind of decision that hangs in the balance in the mid-twentieth century and nothing will play a more important role in shaping it than the policies the various nations adopt towards their international trade and other economic relationships. The decisions we make in Canada will not only affect our own economic future—they will be important in determining the shape of world economy and world society.

The subject I was asked to deal with specifically in this lecture is the historical perspective of trade theory and trade policy. It is perhaps a characteristic academic bias that one should want to look backward before going forward—but it is safer that way. The views that are often presented so proudly as new ideas for new situations are frequently little more than modern versions of ancient blunders. Men in high places, ignorant of history, will tell us that Canada needs new and different policies to suit her special circumstances and will then present, as their contribution to this modern mid-twentieth-century Canadian vision, the most deluded elements of the economic thought of eighteenth-century Europe. We do, of course, need new policies for new situations, and Canada is in some ways a special case, and is certainly our special concern. But the proper policies can only be well built by understanding something of the route we have so far travelled and by appreciating where and why it was that things sometimes went well in the past and, perhaps more often, went badly.

I am going to speak mainly about the large changes in ideas and policies concerning international trade that took place during the nineteenth century. It was during this century that the first effort was made, in modern times, to establish a world economic community. The beliefs on which this effort was based were grand, and liberal, and economically sound. The nineteenth-century free traders dreamed of a world of freedom, wealth, and universal peace. It was not to be however. The world descended, in the twentieth century, into economic nationalism, political isolationism, poverty, and war. The first effort to establish an international economy failed; indeed it failed so completely that there were many who thought it lost for all time. However, the past fifteen years have seen remarkable changes and developments. The foundations of international economic and political exchange have been rebuilt. Moreover, there is clearly more at stake now than ever before in history. Today it looks as though the question of international relations is not merely a question of international intercourse or isolation, economic wealth or poverty, or even of peace or war, but a question of the survival of human life and civilization. I believe that we are ready now to make a new try at world community. It will not be open to us for long, however—what we do in the next year or two may well be crucial.

Professor Johnson and Dr. Smith have been given the task of directing your attention more specifically to current world developments and to the choices that are now before Canada in her international economic policy. I will try not to trespass on their responsibilities or to anticipate their remarks in any way, but I hope that they will not object if I include in my lecture a few comments on what appear to me to be the principles that ought to guide Canada's future policy in her commercial and economic relations with other nations.

In examining what I have called the first struggle for world economic community—the free trade movement of the nineteenth century—it is best that I begin by saying something about the specific economic policy that it opposed and replaced. That economic policy has been given the name of mercantilism. Mercantilism was not by any means a tightly knit, coherent, economic doctrine but it did embody certain important general viewpoints about foreign trade and domestic economic policy. One finds these viewpoints at the heart of the economic philosophies and economic policies of European nations for three hundred years before the doctrine of free trade began to gather strength in the late eighteenth century. In a single phrase, the philosophy of mercantilism was economic nationalism. The purpose of economic policy was nation-building—and this is to be understood fully as much in the military and political sense as in the economic. Economics was at best, only a partner of politics, diplomacy, and warfare, and a junior partner at that.

In this mercantilist policy of nation-building, the chief instruments of economic policy were the royal granting of private monopolies, the extensive regulation of domestic industry, and heavy restrictions on foreign trade. This, remember, was the great era of overseas empire when one European nation after the other made its bid to wear a mantle that had dropped a thousand years before from the shoulders of Rome, by seizing upon the military and economic advantages of dominion overseas. In this struggle for empire, it seemed an obvious truism that one nation's strength was another's weakness, and economics was so subservient to imperial statecraft that it was quite impossible to draw any distinction at all between tariffs and gunpowder as weapons of national policy. Moreover, it was impossible to draw a distinction between the ultimate aims of policy either. Military power and economic wealth were so closely intertwined that one could not say which was end and which was means in the mercantilist policy of European states.

So far as trade was specifically concerned, the mercantilist viewpoint was that it should be regulated in the national interest in an immediate sense. Even at this level, however, it is impossible to disentangle the economic from the military and the diplomatic. Did the British government pass the Navigation Acts so that the lucrative business of sea transport might be reserved as an economic plum that only Englishmen might pluck? Or was the object to increase the number of English merchant seamen as a stock-pile of experienced hands for fleets of war? The two motives were so closely intertwined that they can never be separated. But in the opinions of the statesmen of the time, these divergent aims still led to one uniform policy in foreign trade—a policy of restriction, exclusiveness, and discrimination—designed to bolster domestic industry and commerce, and to hamper those of other nations. The generally accepted view was that trade was what present-day mathematicians would call a "zero-sum game"—a game in which one player's gain is another player's loss, and it is as essential to good strategy to do the other fellow in as to advantage yourself.

The policy of Britain towards its colonies in the new world was dominated by the mercantilist conception, and the North American colonies were regarded simply as extensions of home economic and diplomatic policy. The trade restrictions imposed by Britain were of some direct benefit also to the colonies since they were on the inside of the imperial mercantilist system. However, the system involved fiscal demands upon the colonies which were regarded as so vexatious that the system was ultimately rent by revolt. After the American Revolution, the mercantilist restrictions of imperial Britain became an even greater source of commercial advantage to that part of North America that had remained loyal. The preferential duties accorded to the colonies in the British markets were recognized by Canadian merchants in the timber and wheat trades to be the basic foundations of their prosperity. There was even some primitive manufacturing in Canada of products for the British market, sometimes using raw materials imported from the United States—the beginning of what was to be a long history of American insinuation into the restricted area of imperial preference through Canada.

British North America after the Revolution became more mercantilist in sentiment than the mother country. The exclusive imperialism that Britain practised raised up such protected vested interests in Canada that the loyal colonists were almost as willing to fight the mother country for the retention of this policy as the Americans had been to fight for their independence. The English-speaking press of Canada during this period, for example, was almost unanimous in its strong support for what has been aptly called "colonial mercantilism." There were *some* free trade strains in Canadian thinking at this time. Some members of the merchant class, who were disappointed that the boundary settlement of 1783 failed to give Canada complete control over the St. Lawrence route, argued for free trade with the United States as an alternative. They founded associations and published newspapers but their viewpoint could make little headway against the strong vested interests of colonial mercantilism.

Canada never seriously tried to step out on her own in the developing world trading community of the early nineteenth century, despite the fact that from the very beginning of exploration and settlement in this part of North America, export markets had been the life-blood of economic wealth and progress. We would probably have been content to rest comfortably in Britannia's shelter for a half century more when we were thrust suddenly out of the exclusive imperial nest by a change of policy in the mother country. In 1846 the British parliament, after a long struggle, repealed the high tariff against wheat and other grains— the famous Corn Laws—and with this Britain embarked upon a policy of free trade that cut away the preferred position that the colonies had enjoyed in the British market. The effect of this on the tory merchant class of Canada was electric. The repeal of the Corn Laws, together with the granting of responsible government, destroyed the basic foundations of the tory faith. They had looked to England as the source of all they cherished—the rule of oligarchy in government, and the maintenance of special privilege in commerce—and now dear England was becoming democratic in politics and liberal in trade policy. What breast-beating there was then in Canadian tory parlours. Professor Lower has remarked that it was as if "the centre of the faith had suddenly befouled its own altars." The depression of 1847–8 was perhaps the final straw. In 1849 there appeared the Annexation Manifesto, signed by some of the leading businessmen of Montreal, which proposed the immediate annexation of Canada to the United States. The loyalty of the Canadian merchant to the British connection had proved to be only as deep as the tariff. The tory mercantile and industrial interests have been trying to live down the Annexation Manifesto for more than a century, but it is perhaps not unfair to remind them of it now that they seem to be getting ready to embark upon a great drive for nationalistic isolationism in Canadian economic policy in which anti-Americanism is expected to serve as the effective catalytic agent upon public opinion.

But I am getting ahead of my story. I want to say something about the campaign for free trade in England. It was a very important event in itself but even more significant were the political forces and techniques that came to the surface in this battle over the tariff.

Britain became deeply committed to the policy of protective tariffs and regulations in the seventeenth century, and throughout the eighteenth century the barriers to imports were steadily raised. By Adam Smith's time the list of commodities subject to absolute import prohibition was a lengthy one, and an even larger number of commodities was prohibited in fact by high tariffs. Behind this wall of protection many vested interests had grown up (of which smuggling was not the least important). The various business and economic interests of the community had come to look upon the Government as an agency that should protect their private interests whenever they were threatened by foreign trade. Any innovation in foreign production or transport that tended to cheapen the cost of delivering foreign goods to the United Kingdom market was speedily followed by a petition to Westminster by the affected domestic interests.

I would like to illustrate this by means of a specific case. In the United Kingdom of the early nineteenth century the septic tank and the underground sewer were little known. The streets of the cities and towns had to serve double duty as thoroughfares and as refuse heaps. In Adam Smith's Edinburgh the chambermaid who flung open the window in the morning would shout "Gardy loo" before letting fly with the contents of her bucket. The word "loo" was a corruption of the French *l'eau*, but water is not what the bucket contained. The passerby would shout "Hold your han'" if he was too close, but he was wise to step lively to avoid the splash as the "loo" descended into the gutter. Then, later in the day, the scavengers would come, to sweep the streets and load the filth into carts to be taken into the country and used as fertilizer upon the fields.

Now in the 1840's it was discovered that the birds who fed from the fish so plentiful in the Humboldt current along the west coast of South America had deposited over countless generations on the rocky Chilean islands a fertilizer of great quality. Thus birds came into competition with man, and so began the guano trade between Chile and Britain. The trade was barely under way, however, before the House of Commons received a petition from the scavengers of Liverpool pleading for tariffs and prohibitions against the Chilean guano because their established way of life was threatened by this new trade.

I tell this story because I want to make the point that a vested interest can be developed in *anything*. We always have to remember this when we hear people arguing for tariff protection on the grounds that one's countrymen must be protected against the competition of nasty foreigners who are only able to undersell us because they accept starvation wages, or because they are suspiciously clever, or industrious to a fault, or because their wild life is so disgustingly prolific.

The system of mercantilist protection in Britain was brought under steady attack after Waterloo and it reached its climax in the 1840's when the debate centred on the tariff on wheat and other staple food-stuffs—the Corn Laws.

The struggle over the Corn Laws in England was one of the half-dozen or so most important political and economic events of modern times. That controversy saw the birth of systematic economic theory—the theory of the classical political economists. It saw the emergence of the middle class as a great political power. It saw the creation of one of the most remarkable political organizations of all time—the Anti-Corn Law League. It was the seed-bed for some of the finest literature and some of the most stirring oratory in the English language. But most important of all, of course, was the fact that the free traders won their struggle and succeeded in reversing the whole course of European economic policy. The aim of the Anti-Corn Law League was not merely to abolish what they called the "bread tax," the tariff on the grains that constituted the staple food of the English working classes. Their aim was much larger and more significant—to abolish trade restrictions alto-gether. When the League won its fight and Parliament repealed the Corn Laws in 1846, England entered fully upon an era of free trade. In 1845, import duties were levied in the United Kingdom on more than eleven hundred commodities. By 1860 this had been reduced to a little over four hundred. In that year the great Cobden-Chevalier treaty was nego-tiated with France, which not only swept away most of the remaining restrictions but also inaugurated a network of reciprocal trade treaties that soon embraced most of Europe. Within a few years the British tariff had been so altered that five commodities alone accounted for the great bulk of the revenue collected as customs, and these five commodities were those questionable personal and social analgesics the imbibers of which the austere Victorian legislator regarded as not meriting the benefits of free trade: tea, coffee, wine, spirits, and tobacco.

I want to say something about the Corn Law controversy that led to this great victory of free trade. There are certain aspects of it that are, I think, especially instructive and important to anyone who looks to history as a guide to the present controversy over foreign trade policy in which we are now engaged in Canada.

The first aspect of the Corn Law struggle that I want to discuss is the role of the civil servant. I take this up first in deference to the city in which Carleton University, sponsor of these lectures, is situated. Now we Ottawans know all about the civil service. Our lives revolve around the service, whether we are in it or not. We know that civil servants are administrators and technical experts purely and completely; that they do not make nor do they influence the making of basic government policy. . . . We also know that my last sentence was pure humbug! What may not be realized so well, even in a sophisticated civil service village like Ottawa, is that the policy-making, or should I say policy "guiding," function of civil servants has a long history. Civil servants have been making or guiding government policy for a long time, and they have been doing so more effectively since they became the disinterested technical experts of government than formerly when they were party hacks and placemen.

The role of the civil servant who is dedicated to a certain policy doctrine is all the more powerful when the government that he serves has no such strong views. This was the case in England in the 1840's so far as the doctrines of free trade and protection were concerned. Neither the Whig nor the Tory party had a firm or coherent policy on this issue. This was well illustrated on one memorable occasion in 1841 when the Melbourne government decided to alter the tariff on corn, converting it from a sliding scale to a definite fixed duty. The Cabinet meeting that had decided on this step was adjourned and the members were drifting towards the door when the Prime Minister called them back saying: "Stop a bit! is it to lower the price of bread, or isn't it? It doesn't much matter which, but we must all say the same thing." (This is known as the principle of cabinet solidarity.)

If it didn't matter much to the politicians, it did indeed matter to the civil servants, and that is probably the most important reason why, as

it turned out, it was a Tory Prime Minister, Sir Robert Peel, who insti-
tuted the liberal and radical policy of free trade.

A number of very important civil servants were wholly dedicated on
this issue. This was especially true in the most important place, the
Board of Trade—the equivalent of our Department of Trade and Commerce. The Board's senior officials were doctrinaire free traders and
some of them were ardent advocates of a complete policy of laissez-faire
in all matters economic. They saw to it that the statistics and technical
reports told the right story and they prepared the ground so well for free
trade that the political ministers were left powerless to resist the mounting clamour for tariff repeal.

One of the reasons for this doctrinaire dedication of the Board of
Trade professionals was their close intellectual connection with the
classical political economists. This represents another facet of the mid-
nineteenth-century free trade movement that I want to call to your
attention. One of the most interesting of these connections was in the
person of George Richardson Porter, an ardent free trade advocate and
writer, who was the first head of the statistical department of the Board
of Trade and rose to become the Board's Joint Secretary. Porter's wife
was Sarah Ricardo, sister of David Ricardo, who was the greatest of the
classical economists and author of the fundamental classical theory of
international trade.

The connection between scientific economics and free trade was however far more than a matter of personal connections. Economics was
very important in both the market place and in the fourth estate at this
time. Indeed, I do not think there has been any period in history in
which public policy was so much influenced by the writings of the long-
hair economic theorists as the mid-nineteenth century. The authority of
the classical school in these matters was unchallengeable and one of the
most complete of their doctrines was the theory of comparative advantage in international trade. The most important feature of this theory is
that it asserted the reverse of the old mercantilist doctrine. It asserted
that international trade was *not* a zero-sum game—that it was *not* true
that one nation's gain must be another nation's loss. Both nations—all
nations—could gain by international trade out of the greater total world
production that national specialization would bring about. One finds this
point reiterated again and again in the mid-nineteenth-century literature,
and not only in the technical economic literature but in newspapers,
reviews, school books, even in novels. This doctrine of the classical
economists, that trade produces a greater aggregate of world wealth,
was soon crystallized into a hard little gem of economic faith that easily

outshone mercantilist nationalism—in the eyes of the intellectual classes at any rate. It is rather touching today to observe that evangelical ardour with which this doctrine was advanced in the mid-nineteenth century. No dedicated member of the Clapham Sect spoke from any deeper personal conviction of the pure truth of his doctrine than a dedicated free trader spoke of his.

We of the twentieth century are more urbane and open-minded than the dedicated Victorians. We don't hold hard doctrines in economic (or religious) matters any more. Indeed it is almost an essential verification of the *bona fides* of the modern intellectual that he should feel uncomfortable when he encounters doctrinaire propositions. One thing we should not forget though about the classical doctrine of increasing world wealth through national specialization and international trade. It *was* scientifically correct. Even today, almost a century and a half after David Ricardo wrote, we can only make picayune quibbles and qualifications to the main propositions of this analysis. The fact that it was once turned into an unquestioned dogma by men who wished to use it in a great political struggle should not blind us to the fact that it is still the single most important thing we know about the economics of international trade.

The campaign to abolish the Corn Laws, which inaugurated free trade in England, was carried to success against what appeared to be insuperable political odds, by generating a new powerful force in politics. This force was public opinion, whipped up by propaganda and focused on one point by means of the strong converging lens of doctrine. Despite the Reform Act of 1832 the landed interests, for whom the Corn Laws were such an economic comfort, were still supreme in Parliament. Yet they were ultimately forced to act against their own interests. When one reads into this affair to discover how this extraordinary event was brought about, one cannot help but admire Richard Cobden and John Bright, and the other ardent free traders of the time, for their appreciation of how powerful an aroused public opinion might be and for their intuitive sense for the techniques by which it can be best aroused. I suggest to you that the Corn Law controversy is an important landmark not only in political and economic history but in the history of propaganda. In the issue, it was the anger of men who did not even have the vote that pulled the Corn Laws down. That anger, it is true, was fed by the distress of bad harvests, but the Anti-Corn Law League mobilized that anger and directed it against their own arch enemy, the tariff.

The diffused distress and disaffection of the mid-nineteenth-century working class could never be made effective by itself. England was close to revolution more than once between Waterloo and the Crimean War but there always seemed to be something lacking in the radical working-class movement. When one looks back from today's vantage point on the Chartist agitation of the nineteenth century, one wonders why it failed so signally as a political force. Practically all of the things the Chartists demanded, such as manhood suffrage, the secret ballot, and payment of members of Parliament, are today regarded as elementary and obvious constituents of democratic government rather than dangerous radicalism. Yet the Chartists consistently failed to make their weight effective, in either a constitutional or revolutionary manner.

The Chartists and the free traders flirted politically with one another for a time, and then fell out to become deadly enemies—it was the age-old story of competing radicalisms. The free traders were the respectables of the radical movement, the Chartists were the unwashed. This didn't mean though that the free traders were not prepared to fight the Chartists with their own weapons—including the strong arm ones. When the Chartist detestation of the Anti-Corn Law League grew so intense that gangs of Chartist toughs began to break up League meetings, the League responded by organizing a counter force of able-bodied workingmen themselves. The tables were quickly turned and the League began breaking up Chartist meetings. One such occasion was a meeting in Manchester in March, 1842, at which the Chartist leader Fergus O'Connor himself was to speak. I quote from a letter written by a Leaguer who observed the proceedings. When a Reverend M. Schofield was nominated as chairman of the meeting, the Leaguers in the hall refused to agree.

. . . The result was a tremendous fight—all the furniture was smashed to attoms; forms,—desks—chairs—gas pipes—were used as weapons & the result is something like as follows—"The lion"—the king of Chartism— F.O'C.—knocked down 3 times—has he says 7 wounds—six he can tell the position of—the 7th. was I believe inflicted as he was running away—wh. he did after fighting about two minutes.

Christopher Doyle very much hurt—Bailey—confined to his bed— Murray—ditto—4 others (Chartists) seriously hurt—Revd. Schofield—black eye—loose teeth—cut lip—contusions behind (got in following Feargus) —4 of the "lambs" badly hurt—2 with their sculls fractured—they however are used to it & will soon be well. The damage is estimated at £40 . . .[2]

Thus you see that the Free Traders not only had to fight the land-owning aristocracy who had a vested interest in the Corn Laws but the

[2]Norman McCord, *The Anti-Corn Law League, 1838–1846* (London, 1958), 102–3.

burgeoning working classes as well. The remarkable thing is that the free traders, who were without either numbers or political power, persuaded enough of the numerous and enough of the powerful to their point of view to win the day. Their real secret I think lay in the effectiveness of simple doctrine as propaganda. The League leaders discovered the two leading principles of effective propaganda. First you must assert that what you are proposing will benefit everyone, without exception. This eliminates all the troublesome business of making value judgments and inter-personal comparisons. Secondly, you must have an enemy. Men are moved more by hatred than benevolence and it is a great thing for a cause to be able to recognize an ugly villain. In line with these principles the Leaguers asserted that free trade would benefit all, in the long run, and they directed the anger of public opinion not towards the positive goal of free trade but, negatively, against the vile and wicked tax on the poor man's bread. I would perhaps go a bit too far if I called the Leaguers the first of the modern political propagandists. But one thing is certain—they were not the last.

Now I have been talking about the struggle for free trade in nineteenth-century England in a rather disorderly kind of way. But there is a motive in my haphazard history. I am trying to point out the factors that were important in this first struggle for an international economy that I believe will also be important in the second struggle, in which we are now engaged. These factors are three. First, the views and efforts of the so-called disinterested technical experts of government will be of very great importance. Whether he finds the position uncomfortable or not, the civil servant has a considerable amount of influence and he must, accordingly, decide how he will use it. Secondly, the independent economists, the theoretical technocrats in this matter of international trade, will also be important in deciding the issue. Economic theorists of today do not have anything like the direct influence of the classical economists of the nineteenth century, but they are still important in public debate. Finally, the propagandists will be of immense importance. Public opinion is a more powerful force in politics today than it was a century ago when it pulled the Corn Laws down. Its instruments and techniques have been sharpened and made more certain. Its basic principles remain unchanged however, and it is important for us to remember that doctrines that can be turned out in the form of emotion-generating slogans may be especially effective in the struggle for mass support. It is quite clear, I think, that strong efforts are being made in Canada today to create a weapon of propaganda that fulfils these specifications. That weapon is economic nationalism. It has all the classical characteristics of effective propaganda—it promises good to all, all Canadians, that is; it points to a dangerous enemy—the foreign producer and capitalist, especially the American; and it seems to be able to focus the emotions of public opinion on a single point of political weakness— Canada's foreign trade and balance of payments, and to draw in the powerful ancillary emotion—generating factor of foreign ownership of Canadian industry. This weapon of economic nationalism seems to be springing to the hands of widely diversified sectors of the Canadian public and it is being promoted by numerous leadership sectors of the Canadian community, in business, finance, trade unions, the press, and not the least important, by any means, in certain elements of the government bureaucracy itself.

The era of free trade inaugurated by the repeal of the Corn Laws and the Cobden-Chevalier treaty proved to be rather short-lived. By the late 1870's free traders no longer looked upon themselves as the leaders of a progressively victorious movement, but as the defenders of a beleaguered citadel against the mounting attack of protectionist sentiment. The German tariff of 1879 was the first clear breach by a major nation. It was a moderate tariff but it was clearly protectionist in intent. It was soon imitated by other countries, with only Great Britain conspicuously attempting to keep the free trade flag flying.

So far as Canada's commercial policy was concerned, it is rather difficult to relate it to these broad movements during the nineteenth century, for it was clearly much more determined by forces specific to the Canadian situation. A century ago the tariff was the major source of government revenue and it is hard to distinguish the fiscal from the protective motives in tariff changes. Some historians regard the provincial duties of 1846 as embodying protective intent but even those who would not place the rise of Canadian protectionism so early as this would date it no later than 1859. After Britain's repeal of the Corn Laws, the Colonial Office made strong efforts to induce Canada to follow the mother country's lead, but without success. Confederation, however, did establish the principle of low tariffs for mainly revenue purposes and if the strenuous efforts to achieve reciprocity with the United States in the years after Confederation had succeeded, Canada might have become one of the great defenders of free trade. The failure of these efforts, plus economic depression, led to the National Policy of 1879 which distinctly established the policy of protection in Canada the same year that Germany broke the free trade movement in Europe. In 1897 Canada promoted the revival of imperial preference by reinterpreting the meaning of the most-favoured-nation clause in commercial treaties. This laid the foundations for Canadian policy in the 1930's which was a compound of high protectionism and imperial preference.

To generalize, we can I think say that Canada, though a great trading nation throughout its existence, was never, up to the Second World War, a leader in promoting free trade in the world, but, on the contrary, was as quick as any nation to adopt protectionist policies in response to particular national difficulties. Canada's role in the General Agreement on Tariffs and Trade since the Second World War has been somewhat different, but it is too early to say for sure that Canada's basic attitude towards international trade and protection has changed. That is what we are now in the process of deciding.

I want to conclude this lecture by saying something briefly about the forces that brought about the revival of protection during the period say from 1879 to 1939. This period must be broken into two parts, before and after 1914, for quite different forces dominated the protectionist movement over these two periods.

The main overt force behind the protectionist movement prior to 1914 was economic theory, if we may use that term rather loosely. It rested on an identification of economic wealth and progress with industrialization. This identification was and still is regarded by large numbers of people as such an obvious economic truth that it is commonly presented almost as an axiom of economics.

This view became quite widespread during the late nineteenth and early twentieth century. As an historical generalization it seemed to be supported by the development of England, Germany, and America and where there were exceptions—like Canada—they were not seriously considered. The most influential theoretician of this viewpoint was a German economist who spent some years in the United States, Friedrich List. List's most important book, *The National System of Political Economy* was actually published *before* the repeal of the Corn Laws, in 1841, but its great influence was felt in the succeeding generation. List argued that a nation that progresses must advance through distinct economic stages, of which the stage of industrialization is the most advanced and the wealthiest. He went on to say that this process could be accelerated by a policy of encouragement to national industry, of which the simplest and most direct was tariff protection against the products of the industry of other nations.

The view that industrialization could be successfully promoted by tariff protection was also supported by the most influential English classical economist of the mid-century, John Stuart Mill. Mill was, by and large, an economic internationalist, but in his well-known book, the

Principles of Political Economy, he admitted that the protectionist "infant industry argument" might be theoretically sound. This argument advanced the virtues of *temporary* protection—the use of the tariff to assist a new industry to get started and to weather an initial period of weakness. It envisaged that such industries would soon grow to maturity and then would be able to withstand competition on their own merits. The tariff could then be removed. This argument is an old one. Professor Viner dates it from the mid-seventeenth century. It rose to prominence during the nineteenth century, however, and, in addition to Friedrich List in Germany and John Stuart Mill in England, it was strongly advanced, somewhat earlier, by Alexander Hamilton in the United States. Mill's support for the infant industry argument was especially influential, however, for it came from the very bosom of free trade theory—the English school of classical economists. Henry Fawcett remarked that the protectionists of the 1870's quoted Mill's infant industry paragraph so much that "they seem almost to regard it as the charter of their policy."

Protectionists, however, did not really accept the full infant industry argument. They took the first part of it—the part that said that new industries ought to be protected in their infancy, but not the second—the part that said that the protection ought later to be removed. The argument was a strong weapon in protectionist hands, however—in Canada no less than in many other countries. Some of our oldest industries in Canada were originally "infants" that required the "temporary" protection of the tariff. Most of them still enjoy substantial tariff protection and virtually all argue that this is still necessary and even that it should be increased—the period of their "infancy" is not only protracted, it bids fair to become permanent.

These appeals to the tariff as an instrument for the promotion of industrialization and national economic progress were the most important elements of the protectionist movement of the pre-World War I period. It achieved a certain measure of success, and yet I do not believe that this alone would have significantly reversed the development of world economic community to which the nineteenth century had given such a strong impetus. The free traders were on the defensive in the pre-war period but this does not mean that they had no successes to record. Even as late as 1913 the United States, which had been a leader in protectionist developments, sharply reduced her tariff on the principle of promoting world trade and international competition.

The infant industry and national development arguments were rather weak as purely economic arguments, but through the later nineteenth century there was developing a basis for protectionist policy that was far more powerful. This was the argument for national economic self-sufficiency as a part of a nation's military or defence policy. I do not myself think that protectionism would have revived even as much as it did in the later nineteenth and early twentieth centuries if it had not been for the great growth of nationalism as a political force and of national bellicosity as an important element in international affairs. The revival of protectionism was inseparable from the phenomenon of jingoistic, bellicose nationalism.

It is of interest in this connection to note that the ardent free traders of the 1840's had also considered the questions of war and national self-sufficiency. They arrived at the conclusion, however, that free trade was highly desirable on these grounds. Their argument was that trade would forge economic and cultural connections among the nations of the world, that this would make all nations more cosmopolitan, and thus eliminate war, which, in their view, was simply the result of misunderstandings, one nation of another, and of their common economic interests. This view was expressed as well by John Stuart Mill as by anyone. In the same book that contained the fateful paragraph admitting the infant industry argument, one finds the following stirring passage: "It is commerce which is rapidly rendering war obsolete, by strengthening and multiplying the personal interests which are in natural opposition to it. And it may be said without exaggeration that the great extent and rapid increase of international trade, in being the principal guarantee of the peace of the world, is the great permanent security for the uninterrupted progress of the ideas, the institutions, and the character of the human race."

It was a grand idea—that international commerce would be the solvent of national rivalries and jealousies; that men would find their way, through their common economic interests, to world peace in a world society. It was not to be, however. When the nations returned to the policy of protection, it meant not only the end of the first international economic community; it was but a part of those dreadful events that destroyed also the first modern vision of universal peace.

It was really the First World War that shattered what I have called the first international economy. The war demonstrated the vulnerability of a nation that depends on foreign supplies. The submarine became one of the strongest arguments for protective tariffs. But more important than any specific aspect of the war was the simple fact that the world had clearly entered a new era in which the danger of total war had to be taken into account as a paramount consideration in determining a nation's economic policy. Protectionism became again, as it had been in the eighteenth century, an instrument of national military policy.

It was the First World War that shattered the first international economy, but it was the Great Depression that broke it into utter ruins. The unemployment of the 1930's was so deep and so severe that the nations of the world grasped at any measures to help their domestic situations. In the process they adopted high tariffs and exchange restriction policies against one another, which merely had the effect, in the aggregate, of plunging all deeper into the common misery. The result was the virtual complete disintegration of the international economy.

Since the end of the Second World War, we have been trying to rebuild an international economy. We have succeeded well enough that I think we may confidently say that the 1950's saw the creation of the second international economic community of modern times. Successful international political and economic organization, coupled with wisdom and generosity in national policies, have placed the world in an economic condition that could serve as a solid foundation upon which a world community might be built.

The storm clouds of protectionism are gathering again, however, and they are as ominous in Canada as anywhere in the world. I return to a *cliché* with which I opened this lecture. We do stand at the crossroads of decision. What we do in our trade policy over the next few years will decide whether we wish our country to take an enlarged role in an enlarged world community or whether we decide to shrink within ourselves and to erect national barriers from behind which we will cast fearful and suspicious glances at the rest of the world.

The International Perspective— The Emergence of Regional Free Trade Areas

HARRY G. JOHNSON

University of Chicago

THERE IS, TO ME, a certain irony in my appearance in this lecture series. A little over nine years ago I gave a public lecture in the old buildings of Carleton University, in which I attempted to explain the various reasons why the British economy was still labouring under economic difficulties. My audience, I recall, was rather impatient, and convinced that if only Britain would adopt the principles of free enterprise and liberal trade policy that Canada was pursuing these difficulties would disappear and all would be well. Now it is my task to describe the trend towards freer trade in the world economy, as my contribution to a lecture series devoted to the new international economy and Canada's position in it. But now it is the countries of Europe which are confidently moving towards freer trade, and Canada which is finding its domestic problems a barrier to participation and an incentive to protectionism.

The contrast between the confident homogeneity of Canadian opinion then, and the apprehensive heterogeneity of Canadian opinion now, exemplifies one of the major themes in Professor Gordon's lecture—the close connection between ideology and economic self-interest in matters of trade policy. That theme is exemplified also in the main subject of this lecture, the recent trend towards freer trade. As Professor Gordon showed, the classical case for free trade rests on the economic advantages of specialization and division of labour; and the logic of it is independent of a country's stage of economic development. The adoption of the policy of free trade by Britain in the nineteenth century, however, coincided with the economic interests of her emerging manufacturing classes, and free trade was in a sense a means of maximizing her gains from her leadership in the industrial revolution. Other countries anxious to industrialize resorted to tariffs as a means of promoting industrialization, and Britain in her turn retreated into protectionism under the pressure of increasing international competition in manufactures.

Thus free trade in the nineteenth century appears as an expression of British industrial dynamism. In an analogous fashion, the initiative towards freer trade in recent years has come from the most prosperous and dynamic industrial nations: first from the United States, the dominant industrial power in the war and immediate postwar period, and more recently from the booming industrial nations of Europe. In each case, the domestic economic incentive towards freer trade has been to increase the prosperity of an already prospering economy, by expanding its opportunities for trade and specialization, rather than to stimulate a faltering economy with the lash of increased foreign competition. Judging by their behaviour, nations tend to regard free trade as a luxury they can afford if they are getting richer rapidly enough, rather than as an essential for becoming richer more rapidly, as classical theory would have it. To put the point another way, a policy of freer trade promises both rewards to the more internationally competitive sectors of the economy and losses to the sheltered sectors; it therefore appears attractive or unattractive according to whether the prospective gains to the competitive sectors seem likely to outweigh the losses to the sheltered sectors or not. And this ultimately depends on the confidence of the competitive sectors in their capacity to expand, given the opportunity.

It is not my purpose, however, to attempt to explain why countries adopt liberal or protectionist policies. The foregoing remarks have been offered as a means of linking this lecture to its predecessor, and also to suggest that trends in trade policy have to be viewed in the perspective of the development of international trade and of economic activity in the various trading countries. My purpose is rather to survey the emerging international economy, in the context of which Canadian trade policy has to be designed, as a prelude to Dr. Smith's analysis of the choices facing Canadian policy.

The dominant motif in the recent evolution of international trade has, of course, been the trend towards regional trading arrangements, exemplified most notably in the formation of the European Economic Community and the European Free Trade Association, but also in the progress that has been made towards the formation of a common market in Latin America. I shall devote the major part of this lecture to the emergence of these regional arrangements, and to a discussion of the philosophy which lies behind them, a philosophy which differs markedly from both the nineteenth-century free trade philosophy and contemporary North American ideas on trade liberalization. The regional trading arrangements in Europe are, however, the expression of a more fundamental change affecting world trade, the recovery and rapid industrial development of Europe. Other important changes are in train, most immediately the emergence of Russia in world trade as a consequence of her rapid growth, and in the longer run the effects of the industrialization of the underdeveloped countries. Together, these changes portend a progressive shift in the pattern and centre of gravity of international trade, in particular a relative decline in the economic power of the United States. I shall discuss these more fundamental developments in the world economy in the concluding part of the lecture.

In order to appreciate the nature of the new regional trading arrangements and the change in policy and philosophy they represent, it is necessary to see them in the context of the plans made at the end of the war for the reconstruction of the international economy and of the actual postwar evolution of the international economy. The plans for reconstructing the international economy were strongly influenced by the experience of the breakdown of the gold standard following the depression of 1929, the subsequent monetary disorders, and the constriction and disruption of world trade by a variety of interferences with trade imposed by countries desperately seeking to prevent the loss of foreign exchange reserves or to increase domestic employment. They aimed at reconstructing a liberal world economy in which international trade and payments could be freely conducted on a multilateral basis, and international competition would not be distorted by the bilateral arrangements and quota and exchange control interferences which had become common in the 1930's. What such a system required on the monetary side, to avoid a recurrence of the 1930's difficulties, was the provision of additional international reserves, the acceptance of control over international capital movements, and a means of changing with international agreement, the exchange rate of any country that got into "fundamental disequilibrium"; these were provided through the establishment of the International Monetary Fund. On the side of trade policy, the system required a "code of fair practice" in international trade. Initially there was intended to be a world trade charter, administered by an International Trade Organization, but this scheme failed to pass the United States Congress; instead, its place was taken by the General Agreement on Trade and Tariffs. The third requirement was provision for a substantial flow of international lending; this was provided through the International Bank for Reconstruction and Development.

The aspect of these plans for postwar reconstruction which is relevant to our purpose is the rules for international trade policy embodied in the G.A.T.T. These rules are built on the central principle of non-discrimination in international trade, a principle which has been most strongly espoused by the United States. What non-discrimination means is that suppliers in foreign countries should have access to a country's markets on equal terms, or, to put it the other way around, that a country should not give preferential advantages in its market to suppliers in particular foreign countries. It is worth noting in passing that the principle is not self-evidently sensible—why should it be considered fair to discriminate between domestic and foreign producers by imposing a tariff, but unfair to discriminate between foreign producers by imposing differential tariffs?—and that the imposition of equal tariffs or other restrictions on supplies of particular products from different foreign sources is not in general non-discriminatory, since countries produce different ranges of products and therefore face different average tariffs or restrictions. Nevertheless, it is the central principle of the G.A.T.T. In conformity with it, members are bound not to increase pre-existing preference margins or to introduce new preferences in their tariff schedules, and are also bound to extend tariff concessions negotiated with one another to all other members, on the most-favoured-nation principle.

There is, however, one major exception to the ban on new preferences: members are allowed to form customs unions or free trade areas, provided the average tariff on trade with outsiders is not increased. (Both a customs union and a free trade area entail the elimination of tariffs between the participants; a customs union also entails the adoption of a common tariff schedule for trade with non-participants, whereas participants in a free trade area retain their individual tariff schedules on outside trade.) The logic of this exception is presumably that preferences are likely to be granted at the expense of foreign competitors and therefore are not likely to represent a genuine movement towards freer trade, whereas an across-the-board elimination of barriers is likely to mean a genuine movement towards freer trade. But this argument is by no means conclusive, and the consequence of the exception is to produce the self-contradictory principle that discrimination in international trade is immoral unless it is 100 per cent discrimination. It is this exception which allows the European countries to reconcile their regional trading groups with the rules of G.A.T.T., and the contradiction of principle which has made the formation of these groups—an event probably never seriously considered when the G.A.T.T. rules were formulated—such a problem for the non-participating countries.

When the plans for constructing a liberal, multilateral, postwar international economy were being prepared, it was assumed that the period of transition to such an economy would be short and relatively easy. This expectation proved to be seriously mistaken, largely because of the difficulty and slow progress of European economic recovery, a problem which was aggravated by the disruption of East-West European trade resulting from the Communist assumption of power in eastern Europe and the Cold War. Since the United States (together with Canada) was the main available source of supply of the food, materials, and equipment needed for European reconstruction, the problem of European recovery expressed itself in a shortage of dollars which by 1947 was threatening to drive the European countries deeper and deeper into bilateral practices; the United States, however, came to the rescue with the Marshall Plan, which was matched on the European side by the formation of the Organization for European Economic Co-operation (O.E.E.C.). Both the prolonged period of dollar scarcity, and the co-operative efforts at recovery supported by the United States, had a significant formative influence on subsequent developments. On the one hand, the dollar shortage justified the continued imposition of discriminatory restrictions on dollar imports by the European and the sterling area countries and the discriminatory liberalization of intra-European trade. Discrimination in favour of an intra-sterling area and intra-European trade contributed to a marked trend toward the regionalization of trade, as did the growth of the American economy in the context of this discrimination and the Cold War and the trading practices of the Communist countries. On the other hand, co-operation through the Organization for European Economic Co-operation gradually accustomed the individual countries of Europe to the habit of discussing each other's economic policies and considering the effects of their own policies on other European countries before making policy decisions, thus laying a foundation of mutual understanding and accommodation on which more comprehensive arrangements for regional co-operation could be built. In addition, United States support for European co-operation, and tolerance of discrimination against dollar trade in favour of intra-European trade, rested on the idea that European recovery required a greater degree of economic integration— a concept which was only vaguely defined, but which must have had some influence on European thinking, and which has also conditioned the favourable United States attitude to the European Economic Community and its less favourable attitude to the Free Trade Association.

While Europe was struggling with its balance-of-payments problems, and its currencies remained inconvertible, and its trade subject to balance-of-payments restrictions, a fully multilateral system of trade and payments obviously could not be established. Nevertheless, some progress towards the goal of freer trade could be made through the negotiation of tariff reductions under the G.A.T.T., and by the use of G.A.T.T. meetings as a forum for discussing members' trade policies and restrictions. Five rounds of tariff negotiations have been conducted since G.A.T.T. began—those of 1947, 1950, 1951, 1955, and 1956—and a sixth is in progress now (February, 1961), to which I shall refer later. The early rounds accomplished substantial reductions in tariffs, largely as a result of United States (and Canadian) willingness to offer concessions. But the latest rounds have accomplished much less, primarily because the United States has lost much of its enthusiasm, a consequence of the growth of protectionist sentiment in that country.

Meanwhile, though various European countries continued to suffer from chronic balance-of-payments difficulties, the major continental countries were entering on a period of rapid economic growth, based on the exploitation of modern technology, the accumulation of industrial capital, and the absorption of labour into higher productivity industrial employment. The phenomenal growth of Western Germany was the most remarkable and conspicuous, since it showed itself in vigorous competition in international trade and a strong balance-of-payments position; but the industrial progress of France and Italy was almost as remarkable, though in the case of France it tended to be concealed by political instability and foreign exchange weakness. The following comparative figures for the countries now in the Common Market illustrate the point: between 1950 and 1955, gross national product per man hour increased at the annual compound rate of 6.0 per cent in Western Germany, 4.3 per cent in Italy, 3.5 per cent in France, 3.4 per cent in the Netherlands, and 2.5 per cent in Belgium and Luxembourg; during the same period, the rate for Canada was 3.2 per cent and for the United States 2.4 per cent, while the rate for the United Kingdom was 1.7 per cent.[1]

It was the successful achievement of such high rates of economic growth that made it possible for France and Italy to contemplate join-

[1]These figures are taken from the Eighth Annual Report of the O.E.E.C. (2 vols., Paris, 1957), II, 21.

ing a common market with Germany and the Benelux countries, despite their balance-of-payments problems. The scheme for a common market, which was first proposed in 1955, was, however, the natural outgrowth of the success of an earlier effort at economic integration of these six countries, the European Coal and Steel Community. The E.C.S.C. originated in 1950 as the Schuman Plan, a French proposal for the formation of a common market in coal and steel. At that time, the scheme had both economic and political advantages for France: economically, it promised expanded markets for the growing French steel industry and more favourable access to supplies of Ruhr coal; politically, it was a way of containing a Germany which was in process of being rearmed as a part of Western military strategy. This mixture of political and economic considerations also lies behind the later broadening of the E.C.S.C. into a comprehensive common market, with the political motives—of which the containment of Germany is one, and the eventual establishment of a United States of Europe another—playing a crucial role.

The Coal and Steel Community represented a sectoral approach to the freeing of trade between its members, but it involved much more than the mere removal of barriers to trade in the products it covered. Its activities extended to facilitating the movement of labour, co-ordinating new investment, supervising competition, and harmonizing the conditions of competition. Its success, which was largely attributable to the rapid growth of European industry after its inception, provided an encouraging model for a bolder experiment; its experience with the problems of organizing fair international competition shaped the conception of what matters should be included in that experiment; not least important, its ample administrative budget supported a group of able and active people keenly interested in promoting the extension of the common market concept to all the economic activities of the member countries.

The proposal for forming a customs and economic union among the six members of the Coal and Steel Community was, as I have mentioned, first advanced in 1955; the Treaty of Rome, which established the European Economic Community, was not signed until March, 1957. The treaty provided not only for the formation of a customs union, but also for the free movement of capital and labour, the co-ordination of economic and social policies, special arrangements for agriculture, the harmonization of various conditions of competition, and the setting up of new supra-national institutions—in short, thorough-going economic integration symbolized by the term "common market." Earlier in the negotiations, in mid-1956, it had been suggested that other members of the O.E.E.C. might be associated with the economic union of the Six through the formation of a free trade area. The Council of the O.E.E.C. appointed a special working party to consider the possibility, which raised certain important problems—especially that of "trade deflection," that is, that goods subject to a high tariff in one country may sneak into its market through a low-tariff member—and in January, 1957, the working party reported that a free trade area was technically feasible. The next month the British government, which had earlier declared its interest in negotiating an industrial free trade area in Europe, issued a memorandum to the O.E.E.C., proposing the establishment of such an industrial free trade area.

The British proposal for an industrial free trade area was put forward in "the belief that it will raise industrial efficiency by the encouragement it will afford to increased specialisation, large-scale production, and new technical and industrial development."[2] The proposal was, however, artfully designed to secure Britain the economic advantages of free trade with the Six without committing her to more far-reaching measures of integration, and without raising serious difficulties for her trading relationships with the Commonwealth—or, as a British official would probably prefer to put it, to enable Britain to co-operate in the liberalization of European trade without abrogating her obligations to the Commonwealth. The incentive to participate was to prevent British exports to the Six from suffering a tariff disadvantage in competing within the Common Market with Common Market producers; not only were the Six taking 13½ per cent of British exports, but their imports of manufactures were growing much faster than were those of Britain's other customers—between 1952 and 1956, their imports of manufactures increased by 70 per cent, as compared with increases of 40 per cent in North American manufactured imports and 30 per cent in those of the rest of the sterling area. The fact of rapid growth in the economic activity and imports of the Six, which was dramatically called to British attention by the Common Market scheme, has been a powerful force pulling Britain towards an accommodation with the Six ever since.

Industrial free trade with the Six would safeguard British exports of manufactures to them and permit full British participation in the growth of Common Market demand for manufactures. On the other hand, the exclusion of agriculture from the scheme would avoid serious disturbance to the system of Imperial Preference, since only the 10 per cent of imports from the Commonwealth consisting of manufactures would be

[2]Cmnd. 72, February, 1957, p. 4.

affected, and these would continue to enjoy preferences against non-free trade area competitors. In addition, the exclusion of agriculture would leave Britain free to pursue her own system of agricultural protection, and in a free trade area she would retain autonomy in her tariff policy toward other countries.

The fact that Britain was seeking to obtain the economic advantages of free trade in Europe without sacrifices to her trading interests outside Europe did not pass unnoticed by the Six, and particularly by the French. It was obviously desirable for the free trade area to be negotiated before the Common Market Treaty began to come into effect, so that the two schemes could be established in synchronized stages; and since the first step in establishing the Common Market was scheduled for January 1, 1959, there seemed to be plenty of time for completing negotiations. But despite the fact that in October, 1957, the Council of the O.E.E.C. was able to pass unanimously a resolution declaring its "determination to secure the establishment of a European Free Trade Area," negotiations dragged along. One difficulty after another was raised by the French—the problem of agricultural policies, the danger of trade deflection and the resulting need for co-ordination of tariff policies, the unfair competitive advantage to Britain of Imperial Preference, the need for more powerful central institutions. On all these matters the British shifted ground appreciably from their original proposals, which had been narrowly directed at freeing industrial trade, toward the more comprehensive approach embodied in the Common Market scheme. But in November, 1958, the French suddenly broke off negotiations, presumably because their primary concern was to get the Common Market successfully established, and a free trade area, by offering most of the immediate economic advantages without the commitments to integration, threatened to divert the interest of Common Market members from carrying the scheme all the way through. The Common Market therefore began to come into effect without a free trade area being associated with it.

The failure of the free trade area negotiations faced the other European countries most heavily engaged in exporting to the Six with a dilemma—the alternatives were to work out bilateral arrangements with the Six, or to push ahead with a free trade area among themselves, in the expectation that eventually it could be associated with the Common Market. The latter course was chosen, and in 1959 the "outer seven" countries of Europe—the Scandinavian countries, Britain, Switzerland, Austria, and Portugal—negotiated and signed a convention establishing the European Free Trade Association, which entered into force on

May 3, 1960. Thus Europe became divided into two groups of countries, each pursuing the elimination of internal trade barriers though by different approaches, one anxious to join itself to the other and the other averse to the idea.

The division between the two groups, as it stands at present, and the difference in their attitudes towards reconciliation, reflects a difference in economic objective: the Free Trade Association countries are interested in free trade on the widest possible scale within Europe, the Common Market countries are interested in building an economic union in which internal free trade is only one, and not the most important, element. The division also reflects a more fundamental difference of an essentially political nature—a difference over the question, what is Europe? To the Free Trade Association countries, Europe is a region, the countries of which have enough in common to allow and justify specially close trading arrangements; to the Common Market countries, Europe is a new political concept whose foundations they are building with the customs and economic union. The division has been accentuated both by various recent political developments in Europe, and by the attitude of the United States.

The United States has sided strongly with the Six against the Seven, both because of its recently growing interest in strengthening the wider Atlantic Community, and because its balance-of-payments difficulties have made it sensitive to the effect on its exports of the further discrimination against them that a linking of the Six and the Seven would produce. In adopting this position, the United States has convinced itself, by one of those feats of image-building of which it is occasionally capable, that the Free Trade Association is a discriminatory regional grouping which should not be encouraged, but the Common Market is a nascent nation which should be supported—even though the Common Market promises to be more of a threat to its exports, and less of a force for freer world trade, than the Free Trade Association. The Common Market in its turn has played up to the support offered by the United States, by stressing its interest in lowering tariff barriers, and has given this concrete form; in conjunction with its programme for accelerating the adoption of its common tariff, it has made a provisional reduction in its tariff level which it is prepared to consolidate in exchange for concessions to be negotiated at the current meetings of G.A.T.T., presumably with the United States, which last year announced its willingness to negotiate tariff reductions.

This brings the story of developments in Europe more or less up to date. Two questions arise about the future: whether the Six and Seven will arrive at an accommodation, and if so what form it will take; and whether the discriminatory effects of the progressive removal of their barriers on internal trade will be absorbed by a general movement towards freer world trade through G.A.T.T. As to the first question, much depends on political developments, especially the evolution of relations between Britain on the one hand and France and Germany on the other, and on the evolution of the Common Market itself. My best guess is that Britain would be willing to lead the rest of the Seven into a European customs union, especially one with lower tariffs than the Common Market now envisages, provided that it entailed considerably less political integration than Common Market enthusiasts now look forward to. As to the second question, the answer depends on how far the United States will be prepared to go in offering reductions in its own tariffs. At present it is severely limited by its own tariff legislation both in how much it can offer and the form in which it can offer it, and its current balance-of-payments and employment problems make it very unlikely to adopt the sweeping changes in its legislation that a freer trade drive on European lines would require. But Dr. Smith will undoubtedly have much more to say about that.

In what I have said so far, I have mainly been concerned with describing recent developments in international trade policy, with primary reference to Europe. Before I go on to discuss the trend towards regional free trade arrangements elsewhere, I should say something about the philosophy and the procedure of the European regional free trade arrangements, since these are pertinent to the other two lectures in this series. Let me begin with the procedure.

The procedure for establishing internal free trade in both the European schemes is broadly the same and very different from the procedure for reducing tariffs under G.A.T.T. It has four main characteristics: first, tariffs are reduced by stages fixed in advance, and the reductions are automatic; second, all tariffs are reduced by roughly the same percentage at a given stage; third, dislocations and hardships to particular industries are to be dealt with by special assistance rather than by exemption from tariff reduction; fourth, any exception to this principle must be designed to be of limited duration. This contrasts with the G.A.T.T. procedure, according to which tariffs are reduced by negotiations conducted at irregular intervals determined by the desires of members, bargaining concerns individual tariff rates and not tariff levels, and the results are revocable in cases of hardship. The one procedure places the emphasis on the general objective of tariff reduction; the other, by its concentration on specific concessions, emphasizes the adverse effects of tariff reduction on the domestic industries affected by it. It is this concentration of G.A.T.T. procedure on individual tariff rates, together with the most-favoured-nation principle, which has contributed to the dissipation of the initial impetus to trade liberalization through G.A.T.T.; but it should be noticed that the rate-by-rate approach is a consequence of the form that national tariff legislation usually takes, rather than of G.A.T.T. principles in themselves. That is why, for example, a renewed United States initiative for tariff reduction through G.A.T.T. would require a drastic change in United States tariff legislation.

The description of procedure I have just given already indicates something of the philosophy of regional free trade in Europe. It is obvious that the philosophy of regional free trade must be different both from the nineteenth century and the orthodox economic concept of free trade, according to which the unilateral pursuit of free trade by one country is beneficial regardless of what other countries do, and from the conception underlying G.A.T.T., which accepts the principle that countries employ tariffs as an instrument of national policy and stresses non-discrimination and liberal tariff policies rather than free trade as the objective to be aimed at. What is this philosophy? In attempting to answer that question, I shall have to try to reduce a climate of opinion to some sort of logical order; I shall try to do so in a way which is relevant to Canada's trade policy problem. I should also point out that I am here concerned exclusively with economic philosophy, even though, as I have already remarked, political considerations have probably predominated in determining the course of events.

There are two main questions to be answered: why is reciprocal free trade thought to be beneficial, and why is it sought on a regional basis? As to why it is thought to be beneficial, the chief motivation, as indicated by the quotation from the British proposal for a free trade area I cited earlier, has been to obtain larger freely competitive markets for the output of Europe's expanding industry. Both the size of the market and the freedom of competition in it are stressed; indeed, the Common Market extends the principle of equal access to the market far beyond the removal of national barriers to competition in commodity trade, including in it provision for the free movement of labour and capital (equal access to factors of production), the harmonization of social and fiscal policies affecting international competition, and the control of private restrictions on competition. Further, the advantages of size and competition are seen less in the classical economies of specialization and division of labour that will result from them than in the encouragement they give to the exploitation of technical progress and economies of scale. In short, the main argument for free trade rests on an assumed relationship between size of competitive market area and the efficiency and dynamism of the economy—I say "assumed" because no such relationship is clearly demonstrable from the facts of economic history, and the idea may be merely a confused way of describing profitable opportunities for division of labour between Europe's booming industries.

As to why free trade is sought on a regional basis, part of the reason is that the aim is the creation of a larger area of free competition and not merely the reduction of barriers to international trade; this applies particularly to the concept of the common market. The more important reason is that a commitment to free trade deprives a country of an important degree of freedom in its domestic policies and also makes it more vulnerable to disturbances emanating from other countries. These disadvantages are reduced if the commitment is undertaken only with countries whose policies are congenial and reliable, and who can be expected to be co-operative in emergencies. Thus the members of the Free Trade Association trust each other to maintain full employment and to deal with depressed industries by other means than protection; the Common Market goes much farther, in that it provides for a close co-ordination of economic and social policies, and it has set up specific institutions to cope with industrial dislocation resulting from freer competition and to channel capital into the development of backward areas. Both arrangements presuppose a certain similarity of economic and social philosophy and policy among the members, and particularly a willingness to accommodate domestic policy to the requirements of regional economic co-operation. This fact, incidentally, has an important bearing on the prospects of enlarging the movement towards free trade in Europe into an Atlantic or world movement towards freer trade, and on the specific Canadian problem Dr. Smith will discuss tomorrow. For neither Canada nor the United States has the thorough-going full employment policy and the philosophy and machinery for assisting adjustment to economic change, that would be a prerequisite for a firm and dependable commitment to a free trade policy. Both depend on their tariffs for cushioning against unemployment and economic change, for want of more appropriate instruments of policy.

Let me now turn from the development of regional free trading arrangements in Europe to a briefer discussion of their development elsewhere in the world. The idea of regional free trade, customs union, or economic union has a powerful attraction for the underdeveloped countries, for reasons very similar to those behind recent European developments, and centring on the need for larger markets for efficient industrial development. On the one hand, these countries are anxious to industrialize and prepared to use tariffs, quotas, and exchange controls to foster the process. On the other hand, their markets are often so small and their economies so poor that an attempt at industrialization on a national basis would obviously be inefficient and wasteful of scarce investment resources. What could be more sensible than to join with neighbouring countries, facing the same problems and sharing the same outlook, in a regional free trade area or customs union designed to promote industrialization on a larger geographic base? There are snags, of course: geography and transport conditions and common poverty may offer little scope for a profitable division of labour; the prospective members may be in different stages of preparedness for economic growth, so that the advantages of the larger market may be reaped by the more aggressive enterprises of one of the members; and conflicts are bound to arise between the criteria of efficient location of new investment and the demand for fair shares in the benefits of industrialization. Nevertheless, the idea has a strong appeal.

Proposals have been put forward in recent years for regional free trade or common market arrangements in the Middle East, Asia, and Latin America, but by far the most progress in that direction has been made in Latin America, where the Economic Commission for Latin America has been strongly promoting the idea of forming a Latin American common market. A great deal of preliminary discussion has been carried on, and two smaller-scale arrangements have already been agreed on. In 1958 five Central American countries—Costa Rica, El Salvador, Guatemala, Honduras, and Nicaragua—signed instruments setting up a Central American Common Market; these provide not only for a customs union but for the integrated industrialization of the region. In February, 1960, seven other countries—Argentina, Brazil, Chile, Paraguay, Peru, Uruguay and Mexico—signed the Montevideo Treaty establishing a free trade area and instituting the Latin American Free Trade Association; the Treaty allows other Latin American countries to join. Both are regarded as stepping stones to the Latin American common market. The Central American economic union is obviously too small to have any significant effect on world trade, but the Free Trade Association, and even more so a Common Market if and when it is established, will both give a significant stimulus to Latin American industrialization and constitute a discriminatory barrier to exports of manufactures to Latin America from countries outside that region. An Asian common market, if one were established (which at present seems unlikely), would have similar effects.

I have, thus far in this lecture, been discussing the emergence of regional free trading arrangements. Two themes stand out in that evolution: the first is the importance of the desire for a larger market, as a basis for more efficient and rapid industrial development, in giving the economic incentive to participate in such arrangements; the second is the importance of similarity of social and economic philosophy in encouraging nations to undertake the risks and difficulties of such arrangements. At the beginning of the lecture, however, I remarked that these changes in trading arrangements are symptomatic of more fundamental changes going on in the world economy.

As I have already pointed out, the formation of the European Economic Community is closely associated with the rapid industrial growth of Europe since 1950. The rate of growth of European industry is likely to diminish somewhat in future—the recent burst of growth is more appropriately interpreted as a delayed catching-up than as a sudden forging ahead. Nevertheless, the past and prospective future growth of Europe, combined with the fact that the Common Market will be established over the next ten years, has important implications for future world trade. For the Six will replace the United States as the largest single trader in the world economy—they are already negotiating as a unit in G.A.T.T.—and both what happens in their economy and what their trade policies are will have a correspondingly important influence on world trade and trade policy. That influence will be strengthened by the probability that they will become a large-scale source of capital for foreign investment; it would also be strengthened by an accommodation with the Outer Seven. What their trade policy will be is uncertain: there is a division of opinion between the Dutch and Germans on the one hand, who favour lower tariffs and are interested in obtaining lower American tariffs, and the French and Italians on the other hand, who tend to be strongly protectionist. But they are certain to provide increasing competition in the world market for manufactures, as they have done in recent years.

A second change which has begun to appear in recent years is associated with the sustained rapid growth of the Russian economy—the emergence of Russia in world trade. In the United States, this has given rise to fears that Russia will launch an all-out trade offensive against the West. That seems unlikely to me; but it is probable that as Russia progresses towards the stage of high mass-consumption, it will become an increasingly important world trader, and it may make a major shift in that direction in its next Five Year Plan. The prospect raises another possibility, that both Europe and Russia will be interested in reducing the present barriers to trade between them. (The eastern bloc countries have already protested about the effect that the Common Market will have on their exports to the Six.)

A third change which has become increasingly apparent in recent years is the effect of the industrialization of underdeveloped countries in making them low-cost competitors in the world market for manufactures on a growing scale. The rapid industrial growth of Japan, and the expansion of Japanese exports of low-priced manufactures, is the most outstanding example; but other Asian countries are on the move and the underdeveloped countries in other parts of the world are also likely to become industrial exporters. In fact, there is some prospect that in a decade or so Japanese exporters will be suffering from the competition of low-wage industry elsewhere in Asia.

All three of these changes have one element in common, the spread of industrialization in the world economy. And all three have two common implications: increasing competition in the world market for manufactures; and a decline in the importance in world trade of the United States, which for its part seems to have lost some of its industrial dynamism in the past few years. There is in fact a striking historical parallel between the position of the United States in the world economy now, and the position of Britain in the world economy towards the end of the nineteenth century. Just as Britain was the pioneer in the first industrial revolution based on coal, the United States has been the pioneer in the second industrial revolution based on electricity and oil; and just as Britain had to adjust to the spread of the first industrial revolution, and was handicapped in that adjustment by the responsibilities she had assumed as a reserve currency country and a supplier of capital to the rest of the world, so the United States is currently having to adjust to the spread of the second industrial revolution, and is being handicapped by its acceptance of responsibility for maintaining the dollar as a world currency, and for supplying capital, privately and publicly, for the industrialization of other parts of the world. It is indeed an ironic reflection of the speed of change in the modern world that, within fifteen years of accepting the responsibilities of world industrial leadership, which Britain had long been incapable of carrying, the United States is encountering the same sort of difficulties in supporting them as Britain did.

The fundamental forces of change in world trade which I have been describing obviously portend difficult problems of adjustment for Canada, whose rapid growth from the war until a few years ago was increasingly intimately linked with the growth of the United States economy and whose economic problems since then have been in part at least a reflection of the changing environment of world trade. The immediate problem is what trade policy Canada should adopt in relation to the emergence of regional free trading arrangements; the more fundamental problem is what direction Canadian economic policy should pursue in relation to the underlying trends in the world economy and international trade.

Canada's Policy Problem

ARTHUR J. R. SMITH

*Canadian–American Committee and
Private Planning Association of Canada*

IN A PREVIOUS LECTURE Professor Gordon has examined the philosophy of international trade in the nineteenth century, when free trading principles reached their highest and most pristine academic form; Professor Johnson then went on to discuss some of the more recent modifications in thoughts about trading principles and in actual trading arrangements in the past few years. I am not sure whether my topic was intended to serve as a sort of *pièce de résistance* in this trilogy, or whether it was intended to be something in the nature of a foil, to accentuate the contrast between the clear logic of economic ideology and the muddy reality of practical trading problems and policy dilemmas. In any event I have been set the rather unenviable task of giving thoughtful consideration to how Canada fits into the rapidly changing trading world.

It should perhaps be emphasized at the outset that I shall be approaching this task not as an economic philosopher, but as a practical political economist—not as a person who argues in terms of the impeccable logic of orthodox theoretical arguments, but as one who presents views and considers alternatives with almost heretical disregard for economic theory and "statisticulations." This will, of course, give me the best of all possible worlds for my remarks and a maximum of freedom of expression. On the one hand, it will undoubtedly help to partially insulate me from easy critical appraisal by my professional colleagues, who will undoubtedly be shocked to find that there is not a single economic statistic in my entire lecture. On the other hand, the very nature of the subject I have been asked to discuss will necessitate sufficient general clutter in the topics I must cover to provide almost equal insulation from critical appraisal by anyone in the audience who is not a professional economist.

THE WORLD ECONOMY

Let me start, then, by focusing attention on five key features of the world economy.

The first of these is that we live in a world of economic hurry. This is true not merely in the vastly populated areas of the globe which have been described as the less developed countries in the throes of the revolution of rising expectations; it is equally true of the more affluent and more industrially advanced nations. On the world's turnpike of economic progress, the drivers of even the flashiest models wish to maintain a pace of economic growth that will not appear slow in relation to the pace of some of the newer "hot rods." This is an age of planning for longer-term horizons, of 5-year plans and 7-year plans, of a 10- to 12-year plan for moulding continental Europe into a dynamically expanding single market, of President Kennedy's call to the New Frontier, of less emphasis in economics on business cycles and more emphasis on growth trends and the forces that generate rapid economic growth. Moreover, this emphasis on growth shows up dramatically not merely as one looks around the international community of nations, but also as one looks within each country. Business firms in Canada, no less than in other countries, have become relatively much more interested in what their output and markets may be in three years, or five years, or even ten years. Business investment plans, marketing plans, research activities, training programmes, and many other things are being geared to longer horizons.

A second basic feature of the modern world is that it is a world of rapidly changing technological and marketing conditions, of vigorous improvements of labour and managerial skills, of swiftly changing products and processes. Moreover, it would appear to be a world in which the balance of advantages is inclining more heavily in favour of the efficient and the aggressive, of those who are in a position to take risks and to make bold and imaginative decisions, backed by solid expertise. The less developed nations are hungry for industrial revolution, and the already more industrially advanced countries are generally stirred more by the challenge of change than by the comforts of affluence.

A third feature of the world economy is that business is becoming increasingly interested in the underlying market forces of demand and supply—that competition and price mechanisms are acquiring larger rather than reduced roles. This is true, I suggest, even in the centrally directed and so-called socialistic economies, in which there is accumulating evidence of greatly intensified interest in the efficient allocation of productive resources, in optimum-sized production units, in new and more skilful methods of costing and pricing, in productivity as the touch-stone of economic progress.

In the more industrially advanced countries of the western world, we hear frequent allegations that our market mechanisms are being eroded by such things as excessive demands of labour unions, administered pricing by business firms, interfirm combines, and so forth. But I do not believe that these things have, in fact, generally or seriously impaired market mechanisms. Moreover, economic policies in the postwar period have very broadly created an environment in which market forces have been liberated rather than curtailed. In any event, we can probably expect competition in all of its forms to become stronger rather than weaker over the years ahead. Even in western Europe and Japan, many industries are still undercapitalized by North American standards.

A fourth feature is that we live in a world of greater international economic interdependence—of reduced economic insulation and isolation, of more diversified trade, of increasingly internationalized business operations, of established and active international economic institutions, and of closer intergovernmental contacts and consultation. All the conditions and forces I have mentioned have created, more than ever before, a situation in which any country's retreat towards economic nationalism could be compared with a step back into a box canyon. Such forces are, of course, not easy things to live with. They require more rapid industrial shifts, better economic intelligence, greater economic planning, more skilful and resourceful business management, more adept governmental measures to facilitate adaptation to changing conditions.

Within the broad pattern of greater economic internationalism, however, one can discern a clear trend towards the increased relative importance of regionalism. This trend towards regionalization, it should perhaps be emphasized, does not date merely from the formation of the European Common Market. It covers the whole postwar period. Whether this trend will continue, and eventually produce a world which is dominated by trading blocs and trading giants, is an open question. But if events do move in this direction, it is likely that the world's smaller economies may be driven towards a difficult choice between economic nationalism and participation in a regional bloc. In any such event, most of them, I suggest, will probably opt for a regional bloc.

Finally, we live in a world of political division and turmoil which is not without profound implications for international economic relationships. In the context of the Cold War, for example, there are new imperatives for international economic co-operation and new dangers associated with division. The 1930's showed how closely economic and political isolationism encourage each other, and with what devastating results. For example, there is no doubt that a more politically divided Atlantic Community would weaken its competitive position in the long-range economic struggle with the Soviet Union, just as surely as a more economically divided Atlantic Community would give political advantage to the Soviet Union. Perhaps no less important in the longer run is the need for closer economic relationships between the industrially advanced and the less industrially developed countries. Here, too, political and economic relationships are closely bound together, and closer and friendlier political relations with the less developed countries can only develop and thrive in an atmosphere of closer and more harmonious economic relations.

CANADA IN THE WORLD ECONOMY

Now let me turn to consider how Canada fits into this kind of world, and to assess briefly the salient features of recent trends in Canada's external economic position.

To be brutally frank, Canada doesn't seem to fit very well in the kind of world I have been describing. I have noted, for example, that increasing economic advantages appear to be going to the big and the strong and the efficient. This poses very real economic problems for Canada, both because it has a relatively small total market spread over an immense geography and because it has such a widely diversified network of small business establishments producing on a relatively small (and in many cases on a relatively high-cost) scale. It is tempting at this point to be drawn into an appraisal of the nature of some of Canada's competitive disadvantages, especially since there appears to be a good deal of illusion mixed with reality in much of the recent public discussion on this subject. Suffice it to say only two general things. First, the competitive disabilities that many Canadian producers now appear to be facing should be related not merely to new forces at work in the world economy. They also have their roots in the abnormal absence of aggressive competitive forces in Canada in the wake of the trade restrictions of the thirties, the forced-pace development of Canadian wartime industry when the normal standards of industrial efficiency were necessarily of secondary importance, and the halcyon postwar years when almost anything that could be produced could find a ready market. Over the past decade, we have been gradually becoming accustomed to a return to more normal competitive disciplines. One of the important results is that while there has been some regional filling out of Canadian industry, and the development of a few entirely new industries (such as the steel pipe industry), the country has no longer been experiencing rapid industrial diversification into a whole series of major new product lines. But we have been getting much more efficient in the production of many of the things we can produce advantageously in Canada, especially in the case of a number of products based on Canadian materials and Canadian skills. And this leads to my second general comment—that there is no need for pessimism regarding the ability of many Canadian industries to live and grow dynamically even under still more intensely competitive conditions. This is a point to which I want to return later.

There are, of course, other ways in which Canada does not fit too well into the world of today. I noted that we live in a world of economic hurry. Yet, the Canadian economy during the past few years has obviously not been an economy in a hurry. We appear to have experienced what might be termed a downward deflection of growth trends, and the slower pace of the economic advance complicates and inhibits Canada's participation in the rapid changes that are now going on in so many parts of the world. Just when new technology and new market forces are everywhere urging rapid industrial change and adaptation, high unemployment in Canada limits the room for manoeuvre for industrial adjustments and tends to increase the pressures for preserving and protecting those parts of the economy encountering the most difficulties. At the same time, the existing degree of openness of the Canadian economy places some limits on our capacity to use various policy devices to infuse new vigour and confidence into the economy.

Again, it is tempting to be drawn into a discussion of the causes and implications of the present unacceptably high level of unemployment and the underlying sluggishness of the economy's performance in the late fifties, and again, I must resist the temptation to go off on a tangent that would take me far afield from my topic. But I would suggest that external pressures, working through Canada's balance of trade and payments, should not be assigned the lion's share of the blame for our current problems. These external forces have produced difficulties, but they are not the overriding cause of our present high levels of unemployment.

The most important causes of our problems, I suggest, are to be found in a domestic economic environment which, as a result of many forces, has become increasingly hostile to economic growth. Among such forces are not merely market changes, but also policy restraints and psychological attitudes. Perhaps policy restraints do not deserve to be singled out for special criticism, any more than half a dozen other factors. Moreover, any critical appraisal of economic policy must obviously be tempered not only, as I have already noted, by recognition of the more limited area for manœuvre in policy changes, but also by realization of the need for resistance to irresponsible fiscal pressures and special interest pleading. But surely it is a remarkable commentary on our present situation that during the past year, a short-fall in tax revenues and the prospects for a moderate budgetary deficit raised concern about *inflationary repercussions*—against a background of substantial excess productive capacity, a postwar peak rate of unemployment, and ample supplies of other productive resources. And the irony of this situation is surely compounded when it is recognized that, during the past year the level of federal expenditures, together with existing tax rates, would clearly have produced a comfortable budget surplus if employment could have been expanded, and unemployment correspondingly reduced to a reasonable level of, say, 3 or 4 per cent of the labour force. In short, tax rates at their present levels would produce an anti-inflationary budgetary surplus in a full employment economy.

More generally, the combined effects of fiscal, debt-management, and monetary policies over the past few years have been to produce financial conditions in Canada—particularly as reflected in the uncertainties and instabilities in financial markets, as reflected in the costs of credit to business firms and consumers, and as indirectly reflected in the exchange value of the Canadian dollar—that have hardly been readily conducive to renewed economic vigour in Canada.

CANADA'S TRADE AND PAYMENTS

Coming more particularly to Canada's trade and payments position, I find it very difficult to agree with current influential opinion that Canada, in its experience in recent years of heavy capital inflows and of sizable current-account payments deficits, has been rushing down a slippery Gadarene slope to inevitable disaster. The call to "live within our means," as an admonishment to Canadians to repent of profligate and loose living and be saved, is not very impressive. Moreover, there are sound reasons, I suggest, for a healthy scepticism about the broad hints that if only the prodigal will come home, he may find a fatted calf on the premises. Economic nationalism, I will argue later, is more likely to produce a menu of husks and acorns. And, incidentally, while the phrase "living within our means" is perhaps a rather appealing homily, it is obviously a rather extraordinary expression to have been given such belaboured emphasis by the most prominent figure in our banking system, when one of the primary functions of the whole banking system is to make loans and investments to enable individuals and organizations to live beyond their means.

There are not only many economic inconsistencies and ambiguities, but also many disturbing things, in the lines of argument which have been harnessed to the "living within our means" thesis. Let me mention only one of them—the singleness of purpose with which attention is concentrated on the potential vulnerabilities and some of the alleged adverse features of foreign investment in Canada. Is foreign investment so unreservedly bad that it needs to be eliminated? What would the Canadian economy be like today if we had had little or no foreign investment over the past decade? These are questions which need to be pondered with great care before we ever get close to implementing policies designed to curtail foreign investment in Canada or to harass existing foreign investors. At least among those who have given these questions balanced appraisal to date, there would appear to be an over-whelming consensus that foreign investment, with its infusion of new technology and skills into our economy and with frequent accompanying access to new markets, has contributed much to Canada's economic development, and that today we have a higher standard of living, and a bigger and stronger and more populous economy, than we otherwise would have had.

Having briefly taken direct issue with what I would regard as an extreme and questionable interpretation of our present problems, I would like to take a moment to outline the perspective in which I think our current problems should be viewed. I start with a view of the Canadian economy in the early postwar period—a period, as I have already noted, of exceptionally vigorous demand forces throughout the world, a period of remarkably strong expansionary forces within the Canadian economy, and a period in which the Canadian economy fed heavily on external sources of the factors of production: men, materials, and money. We had a great deal of immigration, rapidly rising imports, and increased capital inflows. By drawing on these external resources, Canada experienced both relatively more rapid, and relatively smoother, growth than would otherwise have been possible until after the mid-fifties. But the postwar era was also a period in which we showed, on the whole, a remarkable capacity for misjudging economic forces and appropriate policy adaptations. In the early part of the period there was an inadequate awareness of the strong, inherent inflationary pressures. We worried about the danger of a postwar recession too much, and for too long. By the early and mid-fifties we had become much more clearly aware of these dangers, only to miss, in an exuberance of optimism about Canada's future, the underlying moderation of expansionary forces at home and the erosion of the so-called dollar gap with economic resurgence overseas. With the unbeatable accuracy of hindsight, we can see that well before the mid-fifties we should have begun to become much more concerned about costs and competition, efficiency and labour skills, and greater industrial specialization. Instead, we have only just begun to grapple seriously with these problems, and even then, amid inhibiting fears that inflation is still a problem and amid a welter of assertions that the high road to the future is one of greater industrial diversification at high costs.

There would, I believe, be little argument with the view that the 1955-6 boom in Canada was an unfortunate one, based upon excessive investment which, in turn, involved overoptimistic miscalculations about the strength of subsequent demand forces. We might well have anticipated that following this boom, with its accompanying exceptionally vigorous upsurge in capital inflows and imports, there would have been a rapid readjustment in Canada's trade and payments position (a sharp decline in both the current-account deficit and net capital inflow), which might have been not merely a cyclical readjustment, but also one accentuated by the broader forces I have already mentioned in discussing the loss of growth momentum in the Canadian economy.

When the over-all balance of payments did not adjust substantially, it was perhaps all too easy and natural to blame the current difficulties on this apparent absence of adjustment in the payments picture—to worry about a chronic deterioration in the balance of payments, to charge that foreign investment was smothering the Canadian economy, to claim that Canadian industry had priced itself out of world markets and costed itself out of its home markets, to urge strong protective actions to prevent "importing unemployment," and even to assert that Canada's national sovereignty was at stake in the payments imbalance.

It must be recognized, of course, that potential vulnerabilities may exist in the kind of balance of payments structure we have had over the past few years—one in which such a relatively large capital inflow is matched off against such a relatively large current-account deficit. As a result of both psychological and real forces, there could well be difficult adjustment processes to any significant disturbances either on the capital-account side of the ledger or on the current-account side. Moreover, there are perhaps also inherent dangers of somewhat erratic and trade-inhibiting exchange rate fluctuations.

But one of the most remarkable features of recent years has been the fact that very significant changes have actually occurred within the payments structure, especially in capital flows, without creating the serious strains which some had feared. Much more basic and important, has been the fact that the Canadian economy has been adjusting, even without much help from policy adaptations, to the powerful forces of economic change that are now abroad in the world, as well as within our own economy. Canada is no longer drawing as heavily as before on foreign manpower and goods; net immigration has fallen dramatically and the volume of imports has declined over the span of the past four years—in absolute terms, as well as in relation to exports and to the level of Canadian business activity. The country has, of course, still been drawing heavily on foreign savings but this is surely related to two critically important background circumstances: first, the maintenance of financial conditions which, at least for a period of economic readjustment, were unusually conducive to heavy foreign purchases of Canadian fixed-income securities, both at the initiative of United States investors and at the initiative of Canadian borrowers; and second, the natural tendency for advantageous industrial consolidation and affiliation in a period of intensified competition and in circumstances in which such developments could frequently be most readily and most foresightedly effected by American or other foreign investors rather than by Canadian investors.

At the same time, in contrast with the import decline, the volume of Canadian exports has risen over the span of the past four years. The result has been a fairly substantial decline in Canada's merchandise trade deficit from the untenably high levels of 1956 and 1957. Moreover, this improvement in the commodity trade balance has taken place without any great efforts to help bring it about. In other words, there have not been, until recently, any significant government measures to stimulate exports (or to curtail imports), or even to influence the exchange rate indirectly in such a way as to foster exports and retard imports.

I should perhaps not leave the balance of payments picture without at least a brief reference to the deficit on non-merchandise current-account transactions, which has been rising relatively rapidly and steadily to become the dominating feature in the structure of payments and which threatens to go on rising rapidly and steadily. In 1960, Canada's non-merchandise trade deficit was approximately ten times the merchandise deficit. Although I have not yet seen any penetrating analysis of the causes and implications of the changes in this side of the picture— and although I am not aware of any arguments that attribute any significant component of increased unemployment to the great expansion in this deficit—I believe that this is a field that genuinely warrants close appraisal. Indeed, it would perhaps not be surprising if such an appraisal were to come to the conclusion that it is in this area of the balance of payments, rather than in the area of merchandise transactions or capital flows, in which there is a real and pressing need for concern and imaginative remedial action.

Finally, in viewing in broad perspective Canada's balance of payments trends over the past ten or fifteen years, it is perhaps well to keep in mind that these are by no means unique in Canadian history. In relation to Canada's gross national product or in relation to Canadian exports, there have been other periods in which capital inflows and current-account payments deficits have been large. This was particularly the case during the period of rapid economic expansion in the first decade of this century, when the payments imbalance was, in relative terms, very much larger than in recent years.

CANADIAN COMMERCIAL POLICY

These rather sketchy comments on recent trends in Canada's balance of payments have been deliberately designed to suggest that there is not a logical basis for extreme concern or for drastic action to deal with what has been alleged to be a chronically deteriorating external position. But they should not be interpreted as reflecting a basis for complacency about recent trends. We obviously have serious economic problems in Canada. We obviously need serious reappraisal of many facets of our economic policies. And indeed, such reappraisal is obviously occupying the minds of some of our most distinguished government, business, labour, and other leaders and many of our most able economists. In no field is this more true than in the case of our trade and commercial policies.

This brings me to the heart of my remarks. What kind of change, if any, do we need in our trade policies? Do we need more protection or more free trade and, if the latter, can it be done multilaterally? Or what trade group, if any, should we join? If these alternatives are inappropriate or highly uncertain, what other choices do we have? I will suggest that we perhaps have six choices:

(1) We can simply go on trying to muddle through, without any very significant changes in existing commercial policy.

(2) We can move towards more general and more overt protection.

(3) We can try to do what we can to achieve a new round of progress towards freer trade on a multilateral basis.

(4) We can consider establishing some form of trade area with the United States.

(5) We can explore closer trading relationships with western Europe, or perhaps a broader North Atlantic area to include the United States.

(6) We can undertake a number of domestic measures which may help to adapt the Canadian economy to changed international conditions.

Canada's trading problems and policies are now a matter of considerable controversy, even among experts who can agree on facts, theory, and feasible courses of action. And the blurring effects of recent public discussion in this field are even making it difficult to state precisely what Canada's present commercial policy actually is, let alone how such policy might best be adapted to meet changing conditions. We have not had any official statement for some time devoted to a careful clarification of the country's trading policy. And it is not without some trepidation that I venture to suggest that our commercial policy, with only minor recent adjustments, has not been essentially changed over the past decade and a half—and that it can perhaps be broadly summarized in the following terms: that we aim to pursue liberal trading policies, designed to foster greater, freer, and more diversified trade, while standing prepared to consider occasional exceptions in the form of increased protection for a significant domestic industry facing adjustment problems as a result of intensified import competition.

But it is important to recognize that environmental and other forces have, in fact, clearly been eroding the basis for such a policy. In many countries there has been an apparent loss of much of the early postwar enthusiasm for the cause of freer multilateral trade. This appears to have been true in Canada, no less than elsewhere, with an obvious strengthening of opinions and attitudes favouring restrictive trade devices. Moreover, with the intensification of competition and the likelihood of further substantial intensification of competition in the years ahead, the exceptions which we have all along been prepared to make to our liberal trading objectives may tend increasingly to become the rule. In other words, even without any basic change in the existing conception of Canadian trade policy, the policy itself may in fact be altered as environmental changes urge increasing recourse to restrictive devices.

My own personal belief, for what it is worth, is that in the final analysis, this is in fact what may unfortunately happen to Canadian trade policy. I perhaps do not need to enumerate and elaborate the various considerations that make it difficult for any government—and perhaps especially difficult for a Canadian government—to undertake a clear-cut change in trading policy. It is much easier to drift along. But I should like to emphasize that "muddling through" on the basis of what appears to be present Canadian commercial policy is not likely, in the end, to amount to a preservation of a genuine policy of liberal trade. Instead, it is likely to amount to a gradually growing web of protection. Moreover, having regard to the international commitments that limit the freedom of action to employ certain restrictive devices, such as tariffs and quotas, there is perhaps a real possibility that this will take place through some of the most clumsy and inefficient devices—for example, through more restrictive customs legislation and administration.

MORE PROTECTION?

This raises the question of whether we should not give serious consideration to a deliberate and overt shift of policy towards greater trade protection.

There is perhaps no other area in the field of economics in which theorists and practitioners have been so far apart as in the area of trade barriers. International trade theory essentially urges free trade, although it does provide for certain valid exceptions. But by and large, trade policies and business attitudes have been much more noted for their abuse of trade theory than for their acceptance of it. For example, industries which have obtained protection under the perfectly tenable "infant industry argument," would often like to have us believe that they have discovered the fountain of youth.

In any event, theoretical arguments would appear to have been of very doubtful persuasive value to policy decisions, at least during recent decades. The petition signed by such a large number of outstanding American economists in an effort to avert the Smoot-Hawley tariffs stands a monument to the fact that trade policy—even when it threatens to take a very unfortunate turn—may not be forcefully influenced by economists' convictions. In the final analysis, political and other non-economic factors, coupled with only rather broad and vague economic considerations, appear to determine whether a country will have higher or lower trade barriers.

But even in these broader terms, there is only a dubious case for an overt move towards more trade protection for Canada now. The fact that there is not a very convincing case for it stems not so much from some of the usual arguments against it—that we must import to export, that we must be concerned about retaliation, or that our international commitments make it impossible to backpedal on trade barriers—but rather from two much more fundamental considerations. The first is that in the kind of world in which we live today, higher tariffs do not provide a basic solution either for such general problems as unemployment and lack of vigorous economic growth, or even for the future prosperity of individual industries. For the industries which claim they need more protection now to survive are most likely to be those which will encounter even greater competitive pressures in the future, and claim that they need increasing protection to survive. To move in this direction would be to run a serious risk of having a growing group of relatively slowly advancing industries—a large rearguard in our economy that would be perennially calling for reinforcements.

Nor should we forget that trade barriers reallocate economic resources and involve economic costs with far-reaching effects on the competitiveness of industry and on the standard of living. The latter is a vital, and often neglected, consideration in assessing the implications of economic nationalism for Canada. One of the most important lessons of Canadian history is that economic nationalism may involve costs which will tend to widen the standard of living differentials between Canada and the United States and trigger substantial net emigration from Canada, perhaps including some of our best brains. Against the background of the large postwar immigration, it is easy to forget that from Confederation to the end of World War II, we had more years of net emigration than net immigration. In the world of today, we cannot risk such a loss of skills and brains. The export of skills and brains is the least rewarding of all exports.

All of this is not to suggest that from time to time we may not need some marginal and clearly temporary trade adjusting devices or even some modernization of our tariff structure. But it is intended to emphasize that in the world of today, more than ever before, we will not resolve our problems or achieve economic strength through substantial assistance to industries in competitive difficulties. Such a policy will merely assure us of keeping slow ships in our convoy of economic progress.

The other fundamental consideration weighing against a more protective policy is one that I have already touched on in the early part of my remarks—the fact that economic insulation inevitably breeds political isolation. A policy of protection can be espoused logically only by those who believe that Canada does not have an important role to play in the world in which we live and who believe that Canada can risk with impunity the dangers of indifference or even ill-will from other nations. In short, protectionism is the gateway to a lonely and trivial splendour.

FREER TRADE?

If greater protection is not an appropriate answer to our problems and dilemmas, what about freer trade multilaterally? Unfortunately for the proponents of this cause, while their arguments are not without considerable merit, the practical obstructions to freer multilateral trade are, at the moment, imposing. This is hardly a policy that Canada can pursue unilaterally or impose on its trading partners. Moreover, having regard to the economic adjustments now taking place in the Canadian economy, it is hardly a policy that readily commends itself in either political or economic terms at this juncture. Indeed, it would perhaps be difficult for Canada to fall into step with such a policy, even in the rather unlikely event that it were now to be vigorously espoused by the United States and Europe.

As Professor Johnson noted, the dominant motif in the recent evolution of international trade has been the trend towards regional trading arrangements. It is clearly of great importance to Canada to know whether the formation of trading blocs can be construed as a detour on the road towards ultimate freer multilateral trade, or whether it will encourage a reversal to increased elements of discrimination, bilateralism, and protection. Unfortunately, at the moment, neither of these interpretations can be accepted unreservedly. But the question is certainly being asked by an increasing number of thoughtful Canadians that if other nations can find what they believe are solid advantages in regional economic integration, why not Canada? In particular, why not closer bilateral trading relationships with the United States? Or alternatively, and perhaps preferably, why not a North Atlantic trading community to include both North America and western Europe—or if not that, why shouldn't Canada join up with the "Outer Seven" or the "Inner Six" groups in Europe?

A CANADA–UNITED STATES TRADE AREA

On economic grounds, and in the long perspective, there are strong arguments which can be mustered in favour of Canadian participation in almost any regional trading arrangement, and perhaps especially a Canada–United States trade area. Let me take up this arrangement first. To be consistent with our international commitments under the General Agreement on Tariffs and Trade, such a trade area would have to meet three conditions: first, it should involve free trade between Canada and the United States in virtually all commodities; second, the steps towards such free trade between them should be completed "within a reasonable length of time"; and third, any accompanying changes in the trade barriers of either country affecting other countries should not on the whole leave these "external" trade barriers at a higher or more restrictive level than that existing prior to the formation of the trade area.

There are a number of persuasive arguments for a Canada–United States trade area:

(1) That despite barriers to trade along the international boundary, underlying economic forces have been generating growing interdependence between the two countries, especially through trade; that this long-term trend has been advantageous to both, and has facilitated more rapid economic growth than would otherwise have been possible; and that action to foster a swifter and more formalized measure of "integration" could bring further important advantages to both.

(2) That despite reductions in Canada–United States trade barriers over the past twenty-five years, the remaining barriers still powerfully affect the pattern of production and trade, perhaps especially in Canada; that these barriers limit productive efficiencies in various industries by precluding more integrated, larger-scale, more highly automated, and more specialized production processes on a continental basis; and that new forces intensifying competition in world markets are strongly accentuating the need to achieve the highest possible industrial efficiency.

(3) That despite increased evidence of sympathetic consideration of the possible transborder impact of trade policy changes (as illustrated by the exemption of Canada from United States oil import quotas), trade-inhibiting uncertainties persist about possible future actions; and that a trade area between the two countries could help to assure that pressures upon the trading policies of either country would not lead to inadvertent or even deliberate injury across the border.

(4) That common defence arrangements and the broadly similar

international policies and responsibilities of both countries need effective underpinning through much closer economic relations.

Unfortunately, despite the general economic advantages which can be claimed for a Canada–United States trade area, no careful and comprehensive study appears to have been made in recent years to assess these potential advantages, to consider what form of trade area arrangement might be most suitable, to determine which industries and markets might be especially benefited or injured, and to examine techniques and measures for facilitating readjustments.

Against the background of recent and prospective world trading developments, I believe that the time has come when such a comprehensive study should be undertaken. But in urging the need for it, I do not mean to imply that such an examination would amount to a simple exercise for demonstrating the advantages which have been claimed for it. Nor do I mean to imply that easy conclusions can be reached about the most appropriate form for such special trading arrangements, or for procedures to facilitate the economic readjustments. Let me mention only a few of the possible problems and difficulties in order to provide some perspective on these matters.

(1) Should such a trade area take the form of a customs union, with a common tariff (on the pattern of the European Common Market)? Or a free trade area, with each setting its own national tariffs (on the pattern of the "Outer Seven" group in Europe)? Or—if they can find a means of doing it—a more "free wheeling" preferential trading arrangement tailored more specifically to suit their own mutual convenience? Each of these poses difficulties. For example, the "free wheeling" choice would not only be inconsistent with the present commitments of both countries to G.A.T.T., but might also set an unfortunate precedent for (a) subsequent inimical actions by their overseas trading partners, or (b) subsequent preferential trading concessions by the United States or Canada to overseas countries (such as preferential United States concessions to Latin America, or preferential Canadian concessions to the Commonwealth). There are many general considerations that might urge the adoption of the "free trade area" approach which I mentioned as another choice. But this might well involve the danger, perhaps especially to Canada, that it leaves too much discretion for policy divergences which could undermine the value and benefits of the free trade area arrangements. In the last analysis, the customs union arrangement may be the only logical choice. But this might well involve political as well as economic difficulties in developing appropriate coordination and harmonization of policies, and conditions for competition

—for example, in such obvious fields as agriculture, energy, and transportation, and possibly also in the fields of restrictive trade practices, taxation, and social welfare.

(2) Other basic questions relate to the techniques of integration. Can it be secured satisfactorily by a treaty—a treaty which would, on the one hand, provide sufficient flexibility to permit adaptations to changing circumstances while, on the other hand, generating full confidence that the trade area will be maintained and not be upset by arbitrary unilateral action? Over what time horizon would the trading area be achieved? This may pose particular problems for particular industries: some may want a swift adjustment; others may want a long, stretched out process of adaptation. Can the price mechanism alone be relied upon to induce necessary and desirable shifts in the employment of resources and in the pattern of production? Would some forms of special assistance be necessary to cushion the impact upon individual companies—to minimize capital losses, or to facilitate new capital investment? What about shifts in the labour force—geographically, industrially, and occupationally— and the possible need for government assistance to cushion the impact upon workers and communities?

(3) A third area of basic questions relates to the possible difficulties of transition and adjustment. Would the initial path of adjustment on the Canadian side be an especially stormy one? Is there genuine validity for the claim that very substantial problems would be involved in reorienting markets from an east-west to a north-south basis, and in basic shifts from short production runs of a variety of products in a sheltered market, to long production runs of fewer goods which would need to penetrate heavily into United States markets in competition with established American producers? Or are there natural tendencies to develop a welter of anxieties about adjustment problems, with the result that they may loom larger than they could actually turn out to be? Incidentally, in this connection, I might note that great uncertainty could well be generated by the mere announcement of a proposal to give serious consideration to the establishment of a Canada–United States trade area, and this could lead to hesitations in investment and other decisions and a resulting recession. If a trade area is to be practicable, it would obviously be best launched from a general situation of economic prosperity and with broad public understanding and confidence in its benefits.

(4) Still another area of question concerns the broad international implications. For example, to what extent might resulting trade shifts significantly damage third-country suppliers? Would such a trade area

tend to make Canada and the United States relatively more competitive in the world economy? Should other countries be encouraged to join? What would be the position and capabilities of such an area in the context of the growing international economic capabilities of the Soviet bloc?

As I indicated, these are merely a few of the questions that need to be examined. There are many others—for example, what about balance of payments adjustments, customs administration, and regional implications? But these will perhaps suffice to show that working out such a trade area arrangement is not likely to be easy. Moreover, in the last analysis, any such arrangement will depend critically on three matters with which I have not yet directly dealt.

The first is that any such trade area must *not* be undertaken merely in the narrow interests of Canada and the United States, without much regard to its acceptability by other nations, and without careful thought to the broad international interests and responsibilities of both countries. A Canada–United States trade area which would be looked upon with suspicion, or even hostility, in other parts of the free world is not the kind of undertaking that either country should embark upon.

The second is that at least beyond the transitional adjustments, such an arrangement must hold forth clear prospects for a rapid and sturdy growth of Canadian industrial activity. It is decisive to demonstrate that Canada would have favourable locational advantages—for example, in the area between Montreal and Windsor, and perhaps in southern Alberta (with its remarkably broad resource base)—for the future growth and development of vast industrial complexes to serve American as well as Canadian markets.

The third is that a Canada–United States trade area must be consistent with the maintenance of Canadian political independence. Any realistic and reasoned approach to the creation of such a trade area must be based upon a clear recognition of the existence of strong traditions of political resistance to it. "Reciprocity" is not a new idea in Canadian-American relations. It has been a hardy perennial—repeatedly proposed, explored, supported, attacked, and rejected. Only for a brief period, about a century ago, did such a trade area actually exist, and even then it did not work without irritations and criticisms, and was abrogated in 1866. Perhaps the bitterest, and certainly the best remembered, of all Canadian federal elections since Canada became a nation, was fought specifically on this question—the result was the defeat of the Liberal government at the polls in 1911, and the resulting death of a free trading arrangement which had been successfully under negotiation with the

United States during the two preceding years. As a consequence, "reciprocity" became, and still is, a highly politically sensitive issue in Canada. But I would suggest that this sensitivity could well begin to wane, as we become increasingly aware that growing economic interdependence is a fact of life in the modern world and that the essential elements of Canadian political sovereignty are not necessarily compromised by such interdependence.

Before leaving Canadian-American trading relations, I should perhaps insert a brief comment on the fact that I have deliberately avoided any discussion of selective free trade between the two countries, except for the rather oblique reference to a "free wheeling" preferential arrangement. During the past year, a number of proposals have been advanced for limited free trading arrangements between the two countries to cover a particular economic sector, or even selected individual industries. As already noted, however, such arrangements would not be consistent with the G.A.T.T. rules, unless it were possible to find particular instances in which the mutual advantages to both countries of free trade across the border would be such as to warrant the removal of relevant trade barriers by both countries on a multilateral basis. But it is difficult to find many ready illustrations of industries for which this might be the case.

Quite apart from the difficulty of squaring arrangements of this nature with G.A.T.T. however, there is the more general consideration that each country will wish to have a free trading arrangement for those industries or commodities which might be expected to benefit substantially—and conversely, which might be expected to create particular strains on the other side of the border. The Canadian lead and zinc industry would obviously like to have free trade with the United States; the American lead and zinc industry would not. Therefore, "selective free trade" is an approach that is likely to involve situations in which some of the difficulties of adjustment may well be especially pronounced. While I would therefore not be averse to exploring feasible opportunities for selective free trade with the United States, I am skeptical that we will find many that are feasible. Nor do I believe that this would provide a workable means towards the ultimate creation of a general trade area with the United States.

FREER TRADE WITH EUROPE

Let me now turn to a few brief and rather general comments on free trade with Europe and the proposals for a North Atlantic free trade area. First, some basic facts. The European Common Market now dominates world trade. The external trade of this group is larger than that of any other country or any other conceivable trade grouping, giving it substantial commercial bargaining power. It is also important to remember that political considerations were perhaps even more important than economic considerations in the creation of this group, and that the elements of social and political co-ordination now developing go beyond even those required for establishing a customs union. Moreover, the Common Market appears to be generating strong forces for pulling other European countries into its organization. And it may be legitimately doubted if even the largely defensive Outer Seven grouping will preserve sufficient bargaining leverage to avert an eventual integration of Europe on terms that may be basically determined by the Six. Thus, I believe that any proposal for free trade with European countries must be prepared to visualize free trade with virtually the whole of western Europe. Any accommodation contemplated with Britain alone, or with the Outer Seven alone, or just with the Inner Six, would very likely be a temporary one.

As for the economic advantages which might be claimed for free trade with Europe, they are broadly similar to those I have already enumerated with respect to free trade with the United States—the creation of a basis for more rapid economic growth through more specialized and efficient production. But there are some additional arguments which are occasionally advanced in favour of free trade with European countries:

(1) That Europe is a more dynamically expanding area and is therefore a better star than the United States for us to hitch our wagon to.

(2) That Europe may move towards becoming a more restrictive and inward looking trading bloc, with the result that Canada may be left like a poor waif on the sidewalk, with his nose pressed to the restaurant window looking in at the diners with their fine dinners.

(3) That there would be a high degree of complementarity between the resource-based Canadian economy and the highly industrialized western European economy.

(4) That many factors would produce greater safety for Canadian political independence in a trade area with Europe, as compared with a trade area with the United States.

But a careful appraisal of these arguments would probably reveal that they are, on the whole, rather superficial. As I have noted, for example, European integration is proceeding with substantial elements of social and political co-ordination, and these could well pose more problems for

Canadian political independence than could arise under a Canada–United States trade area. If Canada were to take the initiative to integrate with Europe, it could hardly expect deference to its own particular interests through significant adaptations of European institutions and of the carefully worked out compromises in the interests of the European members. Similarly, with respect to the argument about complementarity. If this is to be given great weight in itself, the logic for Canada is not free trade with Europe, but free trade with Japan. It is interesting to note, however, that simple complementarity has not been a prime moving force behind regional integration to date—in Europe, Latin America, or elsewhere.

I would also suggest that fears can be easily exaggerated about exclusion of Canadian opportunities for participating in dynamically expanding European economic growth—at least for the basic resource products, and perhaps even for some manufactured goods, which Canada is now producing efficiently and competitively. Canada's exports of such goods to Europe have, in fact, been growing very rapidly in recent years. In the final analysis, the basic advantages would come, as in the case of a trade area with the United States, not so much through providing larger markets for goods which we can now produce efficiently and export competitively, but through the streamlining and specialization of production in those areas of the economy in which we are now not as efficient as external producers. And these adjustments are unlikely to be any easier, and could well be more difficult, if we were to opt for free trade with Europe rather than with the United States.

The proposal for establishing a North Atlantic trade area perhaps derives from a recognition of some of the kinds of difficulties and questions I have raised, on the one hand, regarding free trade with Europe and, on the other hand, regarding free trade with the United States. But I suspect that its Canadian proponents have become involved in some rather woolly thinking, especially on two points. The first is an apparent conviction that its political feasibility would be enhanced through "safety in numbers"—that is, that Canada would be in a position in such a group to preserve independence of action by playing other members off against each other or by helping to form coalitions to resist pressures from one or other of the larger members. This is perhaps a line of argument that has a natural appeal to Canadians in the light of their historical relationships with Britain and the United States. But the degree of co-ordination and harmonization which would probably be necessary to make any such group a workable one might well not only pay rather minor attention to particular Canadian interests in the first place, but might also leave relatively little room for such manœuvering at all. Moreover, even if such manœuvering were possible, it might contribute to a situation in which such an arrangement might tend to work rather badly for everybody.

The other strand of woolly thinking is that this is conceived as a long step forward to the free multilateral trading system which was so enthusiastically accepted as an objective in the planning for postwar trade. It would, for example encompass all of Canada's major trading partners except Japan. And it is visualized as a system that could be readily adapted to include other countries and serve as a vehicle for the achievement of complete free trade. This line of argument reveals at once the inherent weaknesses of this proposal. There are few countries anywhere in the world today that want complete free trade or that are prepared to accept the disciplines it would require. To argue for the proposal in these terms is therefore to greatly underestimate the problems and difficulties which would necessarily be involved in the creation of any such structure, and to neglect the danger that even if it could be established, it would probably be the kind of structure which would be viewed elsewhere in the world merely as an economic underpinning for a military alliance, or else as a rich men's club from which the less developed nations had been wilfully excluded.

In short, a North Atlantic trade area would not appear to be a preferable alternative to a trade area with the United States. And if we feel that existing Canadian commercial policy is in danger of erosion into a more protective posture, with a consequent long-run aggravation of our present economic problems, a trade area with the United States may well offer the most appropriate avenue for change in present Canadian policy.

Domestic Policies to Streamline the Canadian Economy

In my few concluding remarks, however, I would like to take up the question of whether any such major adjustment in Canadian commercial policy is in fact imperative. Throughout all of my discussion of the world around us, of the Canadian economy, and of trading area arrangements, you will perhaps have been conscious of the consistent theme that Canada's great need today is for a streamlined economy—for more integrated, larger-scale, more efficient, and more specialized industry. This is what will provide the fundamental solution for our unemployment problems, our slow growth problems, and our balance-of-payment problems. A trade area proposal for Canada has merit, if it has any merit at all, only insofar as it will help to achieve this kind of industrial growth for us. And protectionism, in turn, founders essentially because it will not help to provide this kind of sturdy industrial growth for a country like Canada.

But to the extent political and other non-economic considerations delay or preclude an appropriate adaptation of trade policy to this end, a skilful use of domestic policies can perhaps do much to facilitate this kind of growth among competitive industries with advancing research and technology, and improving management and labour skills. Such policies would need to be consistent with the principle that we should facilitate many of the basic readjustments now under way in the Canadian economy, rather than bucking them. We might well consider selective actions—such as tax changes, export incentives, research stimulants, and many other devices—to reward and foster more efficient industries with a good potential for dynamic growth even under intensely competitive conditions. But we should not rush too readily to cushion and shore up selected industries encountering competitive strains. This does not mean that for social and humanitarian reasons the government should not cushion the impact of important dislocations in particular industries or communities, but it should be clearly recognized that this is being done for social rather than economic reasons.

There is evidence to suggest some movement of Canadian policies in this general direction during the past year. But economic policies could be directed more clearly and forcefully to these and other related objectives: to a greatly enlarged role for industrial research in Canada and improvements in product design and performance; to encouraging a reduction in the population of business firms in many industries and their combination into larger and more efficient units; to fostering more effective and aggressive methods of distribution and marketing; and to generating greater mobility of resources. This last objective is especially important in a country with Canada's massive geography and mixed enterprise system. For example, an excellent case can be made for vastly extended public efforts to retrain and move workers, to reorient management to new and more promising lines of activity, and to reassess our savings-investment patterns in Canada and assure that there are no significant obstacles to the ready movement of savings to new and more dynamic investment outlets. I should not like to leave the impression, however, that all of this is a job for government alone. We need the kind of aggressive business management which can anticipate and seize new opportunities, and we also need broad public understanding and support for these objectives.

Of course, the success of any such policies would obviously be greatly enhanced if they are supported by vigorous efforts to obtain easier access to foreign markets for those Canadian manufactures which can be produced efficiently and sold abroad competitively. Recent export achievements by some Canadian manufacturers have been promising and suggest that export potentials for quite a number of Canadian products might well be substantial if the present trade obstacle handicaps which they face could be reduced. And great new opportunities are claimed to exist for the large-scale processing, manufacture, and export of many Canadian resources if reasonably free access to foreign markets could be assured. Thus, any programme for developing more specialized, more efficient, and more dynamically expanding Canadian industry should logically be reinforced by a commercial policy which provides a competitive challenge to Canadian industry to penetrate foreign markets and to supply domestic markets more efficiently.

The skilful development and use of these various policies will not be easy. Nor are such policies likely to be painless or popular. But, based upon careful delineation of the particular points at which stimulus for competitive growth may be most effective, domestic policy can also do much to help achieve the kind of streamlining which we now appear to need as a basis for generating solid and vigorous growth in the Canadian economy.

Summary and Comment

H. E. ENGLISH

Carleton University

AT THE BEGINNING it was stated that the purpose of the three lectures was to place Canadian policy in perspective. Professor Scott Gordon provided an historical perspective with his examination of the nineteenth-century movement towards free trade. Professor Harry Johnson filled in the background of mid-twentieth-century world economy with emphasis on possibly pace-setting changes towards regional customs unions in Europe and elsewhere. Dr. Arthur Smith has examined Canadian commercial policy alternatives and has placed these in the context of economic policy more generally. In this concluding section the main findings will be reviewed and some of the comment which was made in discussion periods following the lectures will be cited.

Professor Scott Gordon's paper stresses the reasons for the temporary success of free trade in the mid-nineteenth century and the factors explaining the decline, factors which help to explain the differences in the circumstances in which efforts towards trade liberalization must operate today. The characteristic of the free trade movement in the nineteenth century which Mr. Gordon has emphasized is the importance of ideas. He mentions their use in the controversy by civil servants advising and guiding indifferent governments, by academic economists taking part in public debate, and by orators and publicists such as those who spoke for the Anti-Corn Law League and wrote in the early issues of the London *Economist*. He gives much credit to the latter, particularly for their success in organizing and arousing the support of workingmen and others to support their campaign for lower duties on imported grain. In fact, Scott Gordon has so emphasized this side of the story that he was challenged in the discussion period because he had made no reference to the direct economic interest which the English industrial and commercial classes had in promoting free trade. (The argument is well known: that the middle classes wanted cheaper bread for the workers because it meant lower wages and higher profits; and that they believed free trade would permit them to maintain their competitive lead over their foreign rivals.) Professor Gordon made a brief comment on this during discussion and subsequently prepared the following note for this publication.

To this criticism I would make two answers. First, I was concerned, in my lecture, not to explain *why* the middle classes supported free trade but *how* they succeeded in bringing it to pass, when they did not possess the direct political power to achieve their object.

But, secondly, I would argue that the direct economic interest of the middle classes in cheap bread and free trade has been greatly overstressed. For one thing, the economic theory basic to the argument is rather weak and in my own reading of the literature of the period I have found rather little argument along these lines, except in the form of accusation by opponents of the League. Further, I would defend very strongly the honesty of the League leaders in arguing for free trade on the general welfare basis. To support this contention, I cite the following facts.

(1) The League was, by the time of repeal, a very strong and wealthy political organization. It could easily have been used by the middle classes to achieve other ends desired by them. Instead, the League was simply dissolved when the abolition became final.

(2) Cobden was quite clearly more interested in peace than anything else. He and Bright fought intensely against the drift towards war with Russia in the 1850's and opposed the Crimean War when it broke out. They alienated many of their old friends and fellow Anti-Corn Law campaigners and sacrificed their political careers, knowingly and deliberately, in this struggle.

(3) The League leaders did not cease to campaign for causes in which they sincerely believed. As soon as the Corn Laws were repealed Bright flung himself into the campaign against the Game Laws—a matter in which the middle classes could have little or no economic interest.

(4) It was John Bright, one must remember, who was the father of the electoral reform movement of the 1860's, a movement which was generally believed to mean the decisive shift of political power into the hands of the proletariat.

I would want to be the last person to deny that there is any truth in the doctrine of the social determinism of ideas, but there is more in the sociology of knowledge than economics, and there is more in economics than the profit motive.

In relating nineteenth-century experience to the subsequent events, Scott Gordon emphasized the increasing difficulty of extending liberal trade policy when many nations, seeking to overtake Britain through industrialization, put their faith in protection. Even Britain's ex-colonies, like Canada, became protectionist. National rivalries resulting partly

from this process produced the wars, the failure of post-1918 readjustments and the retreat into more extreme autarchy in the 1930's. By
implication the efforts to rebuild an integrated world economy in recent
years have had to be based on compromise among mature industrial
states and not upon largely unilateral action by a pacesetter with a big
stake in international trade, such as the Britain of the last century.

Professor Gordon notes that while modification of the economic
theory of international trade, especially the famous infant industry argument, provided an important basis for the retreat from free trade before
the First World War, the defence argument became a more compelling
factor in the insecure peace of the interwar years. "The submarine,"
writes Mr. Gordon "became one of the strongest arguments for protective
tariffs." He then goes on to remark on the hopeful moves towards a new
international community. But his earlier argument begs the question
whether defence motives will not yet seriously limit the trade liberalization process, as they in fact continue to do insofar as agricultural protection is concerned. It is ironical that the very massiveness of destruc-
tive power may itself provide an ultimate answer to this concern for
food supplies. If the food supplies which are stock-piled rather than
capacity to produce are crucial in any future war, where is the need for
agricultural protection?

Early in his lecture Professor Harry Johnson includes an account of
the developments which have taken place since the war. This is a record
of the response which political leaders of the leading trading nations
have been making to the new challenge which Mr. Gordon put in
historical perspective. The United States and Canada, with the new
confidence of nations approaching industrial maturity, sought after
multilateralism, adopting to some extent the outlook of nineteenth-
century Britain but held back by a tradition of protectionism within
and the transitional problems of reconstruction abroad. But the recon-
structed countries of Europe have found a new point of departure for
what may be the most successful twentieth-century venture in trade
liberalization—the regional common market. Professor Johnson has
presented a convincing explanation of the emergence of the regional
idea out of the extended mutual efforts for reconstruction, together with
a motivation supplied by the challenge from the east.

Johnson contrasts regionalism in Europe both with the nineteenth-
century British approach and the North American call for multilateralism after 1945. The most interesting element in his contrast is the
difference in social philosophies involved. The G.A.T.T. approach
emphasizes negotiation and develops the attitude that any tariff reduction

is a "concession" adversely affecting a domestic industry, whereas the more comprehensive regional association focuses attention on mutual benefits associated with a general tariff reduction. After six rounds of G.A.T.T. negotiations, the opportunities for significant trade liberalization have been rather fully exploited and there would seem to be more hope for the more comprehensive approach, at least for some groups of countries.

In elaborating the advantages claimed for regional groups, he refers to the traditional advantages of specialization but also to the recently popular contention that there is some special relation between size of market and the "efficiency and dynamics of the economy." Professor Johnson commented as follows during the discussion:

. . . it can be demonstrated that there are economies of scale to particular industries. But a country which is trading in a world in which it has markets for its exports can accomplish scale of market for exports by its access to foreign markets, and the proposition I made was that there is no demonstrable reliable relationship between size of country and economic efficiency or rate of growth etc. What we do know is that . . . a population of 15,000,000 or so in a western country seems to be a breaking point for differentiating different types of economy.

This point has considerable relevance to Canada where in public controversy our small market is often alleged to be a handicap. However the less likelihood of competition in such relatively smaller countries may have a considerable adverse effect on the dynamic efficiency of the economy (and perhaps especially on organizational flexibility) even though it is large enough to support plants or firms of minimum efficient scale.

To return to the main themes of Professor Johnson's paper, he noted that the choice of regional free trade as a basis for economic policy depends upon mutual confidence that a common or compatible approach is taken to economic and social policy. The members of the group must, for example, be able to "trust each other to maintain full employment and to deal with depressed industries by other means than protection." The experience of European countries in working together for reconstruction through such organizations as O.E.E.C. has apparently helped to develop such confidence, whereas there is by no means the same confidence with respect to Canadian or American employment policy. (There will be some further comment on this in connection with the discussion of Canadian policy.)

Dr. Johnson closed by referring to some general expectations concerning the world economy which may affect the success of the

European regional groups, the possibility of the emergence of similar groups elsewhere, and Canadian policy in particular. He emphasized expectations concerning industrialization, and more participation in world trade, by the U.S.S.R. and the newly developing economies outside Europe and North America. Some of the possibilities include increased trade between East and West in Europe, west European exports financed by increasing capital outflows, etc. But one characteristic of the future world trade pattern seems assured—the relative decline of the United States as a trading nation. Dr. Johnson asks how these more general trends affect Canada's immediate and long-run choices with respect to trade policy.

Dr. Smith takes up this question. He accepts and re-emphasizes Dr. Johnson's description of the world as one preoccupied with economic growth. Turning to Canada's recent experience, he discovers this country to have been isolated from the pressures of world trade for much of the last thirty years. During this time domestic growth has enabled diversification to develop, though not always in the most meaningful directions in any long-run sense, because of war and postwar peculiarities of demand. Dr. Smith nevertheless sees this as a satisfactory base for future development which should consist in the choice of those product specialties which can expand in a more competitive world. He emphasizes that only rarely need this involve the absolute decline of an industry.

In this context commercial policy alternatives are enumerated and considered: the continuation of the *status quo*, increased protection, multilateral efforts toward freer trade, and various regional groups. Dr. Smith fears that ostensible continuation of present policy, however appealing and probable, is likely to involve creeping protection in the face of increasing competitive pressures, and that the form of protection may well be the more hidden administrative type since our international commitments obstruct the increased use of more usual techniques such as the tariff. One may add that recent experience—the "voluntary" Japanese export quotas and the proposed changes in "class or kind" provisions—lend support to this expectation.

Dr. Smith is therefore unenthusiastic about such prospects. He sees no advantage and many disadvantages in any proposal for increased protection. Multilateralism must be set aside in a world where the momentum of G.A.T.T. seems largely to have been exhausted and where important trading partners seek other means. There remain the possibilities of Canadian participation in a bloc. Of these Smith favours a Canadian-American arrangement over any other on grounds of economic logic and the possibility of response and co-operation from the other party. The problems which it poses are problems of Canadian political opinion and of reducing, so far as possible, the strains of adjustment. Progress can only be made toward such an event if the difficulties and means of overcoming them are better understood. Because of the political difficulties facing any significant advance in commercial policy Dr. Smith feels compelled to turn to domestic measures to achieve some of the aims which might most ideally be achieved through trade liberalization. He mentions the basic importance of full employment, fiscal and monetary measures, the use of incentives to economize, technical advance and managerial and labour efficiency, and policies to increase resources (especially labour) mobility from industry to industry and region to region. Thus Dr. Smith concludes by reference to policies which may be considered in part substitutes for, in part complementary to, commercial policy.

During the discussion which followed this paper there was for the first time an appropriate opportunity for exchange of views among the three lecturers.

All lecturers were in agreement on the necessity of avoiding the use of trade restriction policies as a means of ensuring full employment. Professor Gordon spoke out clearly on this point the first night during the question period.

. . . there are other ways of maintaining unemployment than exporting it to Japan or some other country. . . . Our international trade policy has to be long run. We can't be free traders this year and protectionists next . . . in my view, Canadian interest, even a selfish Canadian interest, would be to push for an enlargement of world trade and to look forward to Canada taking a larger place in world trade.

Scott Gordon also agreed with Dr. Smith that there is too much concern over balance-of-payments difficulties.

The only important disagreement on policy concerned the remarks at the end of Dr. Smith's lecture to the effect that domestic policies could under present circumstances be substitutes for trade liberalization as means of increasing the efficiency of the Canadian economy. Professor Johnson took issue with this as follows:

. . . it is very difficult to administer a tariff policy which gives you development of your infant industries, protection against the shock of sudden changes, and so on, without creating an awful lot of economic inefficiency. . . . A policy of assisting technical progress, encouraging larger groupings of firms and so on, may simply amount to encouraging the kind of combines we already suffer from, giving tax concessions to inefficient industries, and so on, under the guise of encouraging them to adopt a new technology . . .

He agreed to the necessity of

a few broad measures of which I would say the assistance to labour to adjust to change through retraining, through assisted mobility, is probably most basic . . . and most obviously lacking . . . With that of course goes more adequate provision for those who are unemployed as a part of the process of change. But it also seems to me that unless you accompany this kind of policy by a definite move to freer trade you do not insure that you get the competitive control over the working of the economy. . . .

I would think that you need a combination of policies—to begin with you need to get the Canadian economy in the condition of high employment and growth, and it seems to me that the possibility of doing that exists in Canada to an extent I think unequalled anywhere else in that Canada has a floating exchange rate which can take a lot of the shock. . . . But secondly, you need policies for preventing economic change from leading to demands for intervention designed to prevent change, and I think that needs to be combined with a movement towards freer trade. And in that connection I think Dr. Smith is really saying—While it would be very difficult to negotiate such a thing, we are agreed that the logical direction for such a move to go is towards freer trade with the United States.

As the reading of the lectures will confirm, there was not as much disagreement among the lecturers as the first section of these remarks might imply. Dissent lay mainly in a difference in emphasis concerning the intractability of trade policy.

Out of the three lectures there then emerges the picture of a world economy proceeding on familiar theoretical economic grounds towards a widely applauded objective of freedom of trade, but for practical reasons employing new means—the regional free trade group. It is suggested that such a method may have wider applicability and that indeed it might be appropriate for North America. It remains uncertain whether such groups will in fact be a stage in the development of freer trade between regions as well as within regions. For Canada, either way, it is increasingly clear that a world of more vigorous competition and healthier regional economies will require some new venture in commercial policy as an alternative to the misfortune of economic isolation.

Lightning Source UK Ltd.
Milton Keynes UK
UKHW010014210722
406167UK00002B/456